Eves' ar...

The
90 −minute
manager

Books to make you better

Books to make you better. To make you *be* better, *do* better, *feel* better. Whether you want to upgrade your personal skills or change your job, whether you want to improve your managerial style, become a more powerful communicator, or be stimulated and inspired as you work.

Prentice Hall Business is leading the field with a new breed of skills, careers and development books. Books that are a cut above the mainstream – in topic, content and delivery – with an edge and verve that will make you better, with less effort.

Books that are as sharp and smart as you are.

Prentice Hall Business.
We work harder – so you don't have to.

For more details on products, and to contact us, visit
www.business-minds.com
www.yourmomentum.com

David Bolchover &
Chris Brady

The 90 -minute manager

Business lessons from the dugout

Prentice
Hall

BUSINESS

an imprint of **Pearson Education**

London • New York • Toronto • Sydney • Tokyo • Singapore

Hong Kong • Cape Town • New Delhi • Madrid • Paris

Amsterdam • Munich • Milan • Stockholm

PEARSON EDUCATION LIMITED

Head Office:
Edinburgh Gate
Harlow CM20 2JE
Tel: +44 (0)1279 623623
Fax: +44 (0)1279 431059

London Office:
128 Long Acre
London WC2E 9AN
Tel: +44 (0)20 7447 2000
Fax: +44 (0)20 7240 5771
Website: www.business-minds.com

First published in Great Britain in 2002

© Pearson Education Limited 2002

The rights of David Bolchover and Chris Brady to be identified as Authors of this Work have been asserted by them in accordance with the Copyright, Designs and Patents Act 1988.

ISBN 0 273 65613 9

British Library Cataloguing in Publication Data
A CIP catalogue record for this book can be obtained from the British Library

10 9 8 7 6 5

Designed by Claire Brodmann Book Designs, Lichfield, Staffs.
Typeset by Northern Phototypesetting Co. Ltd, Bolton
Printed and bound in Great Britain by Biddles Ltd, Guildford and King's Lynn

The Publishers' policy is to use paper manufactured from sustainable forests.

Dedication

To the memories of
Anthony Bolchover and Yank Albers

Acknowledgements

We would like to thank a number of people for their help in completing this book. Pete Shemilt, at Pearson, who first proposed turning the idea into a book; Rachael Stock, our publisher, who never wavered in her support for the project; David Benson, Paul Frankland and Robin Shepherd, who each provided invaluable feedback on several chapters; Colm O'Sullivan, Will Rosen, David Taylor and Nic Wilmot for some extremely useful suggestions and ideas; Rebecca Southin who helped with manuscripts and never yawned in public; and countless others for their insights and encouragement.

Contents

PART I

Parallels

I'm saying that people are people, and that the keys
to motivating them and getting them to perform to
their full potential are pretty much the same
whether they're playing on a football field or
working in an office.

Bill Parcells, NFL coach

Football is <u>the</u> model

REVIEWS OF MANAGEMENT BOOKS NORMALLY CONTAIN AN OPENING sentence something like, 'here we go again, another fatuous attempt to spice up the mundaneness of real business management with forced metaphors from the sporting world'. Whatever else reviewers may think of this book, they must not mistake it for an extended metaphor. This book shows that football is a *model*, not simply a metaphor, for contemporary knowledge-based businesses. As such it provides unique insights into the crucial management issues confronting the modern corporate environment. Football has been neglected as a model for too long, primarily, we believe, because of its working-class roots and consequent inaccessibility for the usual business book audience.

Well, football is sexy now and in becoming so it has simultaneously become an accessible model for those with an interest in business. Football itself has, as the world game, always been accessible to the vast majority of the world's population, but never in the rarefied atmosphere inhabited by senior business people. Even politicians no longer hide their allegiances, instead they boast about them. The Prime Minister even invents them. Sir Richard Greenbury, former chairman of Marks and Spencer, refers to Manchester United manager Alex Ferguson as the best man-manager in British industry, and Jurgen Schrempp, chairman of DaimlerChrysler, has named Ottmar Hitzfield (Bayern

Munich) as the model for German business managers. Aime Jacquet brought an entire nation together winning the World Cup for, and in, France. He was lauded by his nation's president at a victory rally which brought more people on to the streets of Paris than were there at the end of the Second World War.

Lessons provided by this newly accessible model of football could not be more timely. For example, in 2000, M. Douglas Ivester was sacked as the chief executive officer (CEO) of Coca-Cola. He had gone almost before the body of Roberto Goizueta, his predecessor, was cold. It was not an isolated instance of what has become known as 'CEO-churning'. A report by FT Dynamo, the now defunct online forum of the *Financial Times*, found that in February 2001 alone, 119 CEOs in the US left their jobs. Since 1995, one-third of Fortune 100 companies have replaced their CEOs. A quarter of all CEO appointees fail to see out their contracts for one reason or another. A Sloan Business School report also showed that CEOs appointed post-1985 were three times more likely to be fired than their pre-1985 counterparts.

Why has the lot of the CEO become so precarious, albeit so rewarding? According to Jeffrey Garten, the Dean of Yale Business School, there are three powerful reasons:

- the sheer difficulty of running a multinational company during a time of tremendous technological change;
- the great uncertainties of the global environment;
- the need for a CEO to be both a business leader and a global statesman concerned with everything from environmental protection to rules for cyberspace.

Although the list sounds plausible, it is wrong. The current spate of technological changes is relatively insignificant when compared with the invention of cheap electricity, telephones, tele-

graph, the train, the plane, the internal combustion engine, the fridge – the list goes on. Similarly, the issues of environmental turbulence and the businessman/statesman demands are nothing new. These are generic pressures that all leaders of large organizations have always faced.

What *has* exacerbated the pressures, however, is the recognition of the power of the investors, *by* those investors. It is their continual and increasingly vociferous demands for increased and sustained growth in share performance that has changed the life of the corporate CEO into the precarious position it is now. In other words, business leaders are arriving where football managers have always been, at the mercy of a constituency of disparate and demanding stakeholders.

In a special supplement of *The Economist* (3 November 2001), the management guru Peter Drucker precisely illustrated the management dilemma in the modern knowledge-based business world. Drucker argued that knowledge has become the global currency. Why? Because it has the attributes of currency. It is fluid, crosses

> Business leaders are arriving where football managers have always been.

boundaries and is scarce. Capital, in the traditional sense, therefore, has become a commodity and today's real corporate issue is not to raise money but to recruit those who own the new capital.

Following Drucker's logic, if knowledge is the new capital then 'knowledge workers, collectively, are the new capitalists [because] they own the means of production'. The key word in that quote is 'collectively'. Why? Because knowledge workers can leverage their capital (knowledge) only if they have access to some form of organization that can assemble an array of know-

ledge workers in order to direct their special talents towards a common goal. Even sole traders and entrepreneurs who use knowledge cannot operate in a vacuum: they too require a regulated market place.

Such organizations will provide enormous managerial challenges because the traditional hierarchical boss/subordinate relationships will have to change. The knowledge organizations will be organizations of equals, in the professional sense. The manager will be authorized by the professionals to take on the role of co-ordinator, or 'ringmaster', because it will be recognized that the manager's skills, as a manager, will add value both to the organization and to individuals within the organization.

WHY FOOTBALL?

The role that modern business managers are increasingly being asked to play is precisely the same one that football managers have always played. They have always been the 'ringmaster' trying to channel the activities of talented individuals for the corporate good. They have always been at the mercy of a variety of conflicting stakeholder demands, not least of which have been those of the players. Once a football manager loses the authority of the players, his position is untenable.

In a fascinating interview in *Strategy and Business* (Rothenburg, 2001) with the 'guru of organizational learning', Arie de Geus, a very explicit link is made between football and modern business management issues. De Geus focuses on the tension between legitimate shareholder demands and the needs of those he calls the 'members of the work community'. The shareholders quite reasonably, and legally, claim a 'right to the bottom line'; the knowledge workers, equally reasonably, respond that 'that there is

no bottom line without our talent'. The interviewer asked de Geus if he saw a model for the resolution of such conflict. De Geus replied:

> ❝I am very intrigued by the example of one particular group of – let's call them human associations – where the conflict is nakedly visible. These are the European football clubs.❞

De Geus went on to draw lessons from the management of the entirety of the football club as a business but he also accepted that the football itself, being the core of the business, is the most valuable focus of any analysis.

Business is, actually, making the journey football did many years ago. It is the journey towards the ultimate realization of the importance of the manager. The realization is occurring because performance in business at all levels is gradually becoming as open to scrutiny and analysis as football has always been. In a football team, a good manager is easy to identify, because his team consistently achieves results. In a large company, good managers have been difficult to identify, often lost in the fog of corporate politics and bureaucracy. This lack of openness damages management performance because it provides little incentive for good managers to be rewarded or bad ones punished. It precludes meritocracy and leads to cronyism. Growing external pressures are now forcing internal company operations to become increasingly professional, so that management performance will be more measurable and the positive effect of a consistently good manager more obvious. Cynics in business may scoff at the idea of learning from the experience of football but they do so at their peril because business is moving towards the openness and visibility which football has always possessed.

Managing an elite football team also replicates all the problems of corporate management in the global environment. Consider for a moment the composition of the Chelsea football team one Saturday in the 1999/2000 season. It was a team managed by an Italian, coached by an Englishman, with a combination of English, French, Italian, Dutch, Spanish, Uruguayan, Brazilian, Finnish, Romanian, Norwegian and Nigerian players. Not only were these players of different nationalities, they were also culturally diverse. Gianluca Vialli, the manager, is from an extremely wealthy family; Marcel Desailly, the central defender, is from a poor background, is black and was born in Accra, Ghana; his French compatriot and central-defensive partner, Frank Leboeuf, is from a rural background and is white. The Finnish striker, Mikael Forssell, is 18 years old and the Romanian, Dan Petrescu, is in his thirties. Also consider that the average tenure for Premier League managers is about 39 months; for FTSE 100 CEOs it is about 45 months.

Not only does football replicate the problems, it intensifies them and then accelerates the process by compressing the timescale and sharpening the focus. Mostly this is a result of the relentless nature of media attention. As Manchester City's chairman said:

In football virtually everything is on view; what is not on immediate show is soon revealed by almost permanent media attention.

'In football you have at least 40 AGMs every year, each with 40,000 shareholders.' A single moment, one slip from a player, can cost a manager his job. What football provides is a pure model of corporate management where *only* best practice succeeds. It is, therefore, easier to identify and analyze that best practice. Furthermore, its visibility is total.

We cannot easily dissect the behaviour of the top CEOs in real time because so much remains secret for so long. By contrast, in football virtually everything is on view; what is not on immediate show is soon revealed by almost permanent media attention.

Orchestral manoeuvres

In 1988, Peter Drucker wrote an article in the *Harvard Business Review* called 'The coming of the new organization'. In the process of deconstructing the 'old' organization Drucker suggested that the most appropriate model for the 'new' organization was the orchestra. An orchestra, with its disparate, highly skilled individuals, all focused on the same objective, seemed to provide an insightful metaphor for process-centred organizations. An orchestra was, according to Drucker, a group full of high-level specialists (i.e. knowledge workers) under the overall leadership of the charismatic conductor.

Later, other gurus, such as Henry Mintzberg, were to refine the orchestra metaphor even further. The problem is that as seductive as the metaphor is, it is wrong. An orchestra rehearses and executes under static conditions. Other orchestras do not interrupt or disrupt the execution of the performance. The programme of pieces will not be altered mid-performance, the first violinist will not be asked to jump in and cover for the second trombone. It is precisely this lack of fluidity between roles which so fundamentally disqualifies the orchestra as a metaphor for modern businesses.

Just as significantly, the pool of talent from which to select orchestra members is, if not inexhaustible, certainly relatively deep. There are as many waiter/musicians as there are waiter/actors. The inadequacies of the orchestra metaphor are

the same as those of the acting ensemble metaphor. While initially attractive, ultimately these metaphors do not survive detailed scrutiny. They have powerful but limited utility. For example, they have value when related to fixed-term project management, but little else. The main reason such metaphors proliferated was that they appealed to the middle classes which traditionally dominated both the corporate and academic domains.

Just as elitist metaphors appealed to elitist analysts, so working-class metaphors were ignored. As a consequence, sports of the British middle classes, such as rugby union, provided fertile ground for business management books. So much so that the *Living with the Lions* video of the 1997 Lions' tour of South Africa became almost compulsory viewing for management seminars. While the McGeechan/Telfer (the tour's coach/assistant coach) brand of management clearly had powerful lessons for fixed-term project management, it too failed to provide any genuine insights into the day-to-day pressures facing key decision makers in the corporate world.

Where it also failed, as did the orchestra metaphor, was in replicating the structural subtleties of modern business. Rugby Union, at least at that stage, was characterized by rigid functional demarcation; not as rigid as American football with its offensive, defensive and special teams, but nevertheless quite restrictive. The idea of mobile, try-scoring forwards in the George Smith, Keith Wood, Lawrence Dallaglio mould was unheard of. The notion of interchangeable players seemed light years away.

In contrast to this rigidly functionalist structure, business was moving towards flatter organizations accommodating multiple-functioned and highly skilled individuals able to cover colleagues called away on priority tasks. Ironically, the 2001 Lions' tour to

Australia demonstrated, both on and off the field, a more flexible attitude towards interchangeability. Notwithstanding the change in attitude, a rugby union tour still most closely resembles fixed-term project management. As such it requires specific management techniques. Bringing together a team for a specific length of time in order to achieve specific goals, which will automatically enhance the value of individuals, demands certain skills of a manager but they do not compare with the skills needed to sustain success over an unlimited timescale.

Management techniques

The techniques of tour management are similar to those needed for international football management. The difference between league and international management is what makes the appointment of international managers such a risky business. Almost by definition very few have international experience. Interestingly, there is a small coterie of managers with international expertise who ply their trade around the developing football nations. The Yugoslav Bora Milutinovic, for example, has managed five nations to the World Cup finals: Mexico in 1986, Costa Rica in 1990, the US in 1994, Nigeria in 1998 and China in 2002.

League management, however, is an altogether greater challenge. It requires that a team is managed on an ongoing basis, continually producing performance at a level which constitutes success. It also requires managers who are able to reproduce their success with other teams when they either resign or are sacked by their current employers. If that sounds familiar, then it should do. It's the role played by modern CEOs. They too are required to manage teams which are made up of highly skilled and highly sought-after individuals. The CEOs are ultimately responsible for the success or failure of the organization. Their 'players' may be

management consultants, sales people, computer whizzes, financial experts or product specialists, but they need *managing* to ensure that the organization (the team) succeeds.

Reports on the 'talent war' by management consulting firm McKinsey showed that 'companies scoring in the top quintile of talent-management practices outperform their industry's mean return to shareholders by a remarkable 22 percentage points'. Football is clearly not just a metaphor for the new knowledge industry, football is the *model*. Had football been an American sport it would have been the dominant model for business management years ago. In the US the mass sports tend to be classless and their analogous powers are, therefore, accessible to everybody. In 1985 American writer Robert Keidel wrote a book entitled *Game Plans* in which he established clear structural links with the business world. He argued that 'the three major team sports in the United States – baseball, football and basketball – represent generic organizational forms common in business (and other sectors)'. In his book, Keidel makes the point that, of the sports he investigated, it was basketball that was the most concentrated and complex and where the players were 'connected to all their team-mates in a fluid manner'.

> Had football been an American sport it would have been the dominant model for business management years ago.

By contrast, the basic units in American football are issue-specific (functional) sub-teams and in baseball they are individuals. In basketball, the basic unit *is* the team. This is also true of football, only more so. In addition to the fluidity of basketball, soccer has the set-plays associated with American football as well as the

same number of players on the pitch as American football. Thus soccer has both the fluidity of basketball and the structured pre-programming of American football. In fact, the transitional nature of soccer, in which players are instantaneously trans-formed from attackers to defenders and vice versa, most accu-rately reflects the dynamism of contemporary corporate organizations. Football truly is the management of independence, which is also the cornerstone of modern information-rich organ-izations.

The issues that confront modern organizations are precisely the issues which confront football teams. Those issues include the debate concerning the separation of duties between CEOs and chairmen, the so-called 'talent war', the development of a strate-gic direction, the creation of tactical plans, the continuity and succession of managers, the relationships between CEOs and their chairman, their shareholders, the media and the regulatory authorities – these are all relationships which are central to both business and football.

For example, one lesson that football so readily provides – and one that new football managers have to learn very early – is that they can no longer play. Their job is to design the playing pattern (the process) and to co-ordinate the players to implement the pattern. The co-ordinators must then observe and monitor the performance (feedback), assess the performance, redesign the process – and improve or remove the players. Only in that way can teams (organizations) continue to improve.

However – and this is where football is imitating business – the co-ordinator's job is no longer synonymous with that of the man-ager. Not only can they no longer play, they do not have time even to coach. When Dennis Green was appointed head coach of the NFL team the Minnesota Vikings in the mid-1990s, he was asked what he missed most in his new role as head coach. 'Coaching,' he replied. Just as in business, Premier League managers have a senior management team working under them. To a certain extent some of them still have difficulty in coming to terms with this reality. There is still a first-team coach, reserve coach and youth coach, whereas football might be better served by the use of American terminology such as head coach, offensive and defensive co-ordinators, and position coaches. Whatever the nomenclature, the jobs are the same. The manager (head coach) is responsible for the values and culture around which the other members of the management team and the players converge for direction.

Those who doubt the importance of the manager, or the CEO, need only look at those teams which continue to succeed despite changes in the playing staff. At Manchester United, for example, it is easy to forget that ten years ago, the right and left flank positions were the preserve of Andrei Kanchelskis and Lee Sharpe. The transition to David Beckham and Ryan Giggs was seamlessly *managed*. Alex Ferguson does not personally coach individual players but he sets the tone and the standards. When Sharpe, for example, fell below those standards, especially off the field, he was moved on.

Another indicator of managerial significance is the way in which a team can be turned around with virtually the same players. Martin O'Neill's early success at Celtic is a classic example. In football, as in business, the skill sets of the players are virtually indistinguishable; what makes the difference is the manager. It is the manager's responsibility to ensure that the potential of each player is realized *through* the team and *for* the team.

The art of management

If it were not true that the manager makes a difference or at least is perceived to do so, why pay such exorbitant salaries and bonuses? The answer, of course, is that it *is* true. More precisely, it *can* be true, which is the problem. Despite constant attempts to establish management as a science, it is clearly more of an art. That does not mean that it cannot be analyzed and that best practice cannot be drawn from such analysis. Picking the right manager is the most value that a chairman can add to a football club and picking the right CEO is the most value that a chairman of a company can add to that business. Reference to football shows us that the two jobs must be separated. Even Ron Noades, who was initially successful in combining the jobs of chairman and manager at Brentford, was soon forced to relinquish the manager's job.

Peter Ridsdale, the chairman of Leeds United, has been particularly successful at picking managers so far. He picked both George Graham and David O'Leary. The latter was, admittedly, second choice to Martin O'Neill, who probably would have taken the job if he had been allowed to speak to the Leeds chairman. He wasn't, and O'Leary has had initial success in the job. He has also had the complete backing of the chairman, to the extent that in November 2000 Leeds spent £18 million on central defender Rio Ferdinand at a time when others were waiting to see what the fall-out from EU legislation would be on the transfer market.

This simple triangular relationship between chairman, manager and legislature (those who run the game) is just one sub-set of the complex matrix of relationships that managers and CEOs must handle. A fuller indication of this complexity is shown in Figure 1.1, although it too can only be partial.

Figure 1.1 The complex network of relationships that managers and CEOs must handle

What is clear is the validity of football as the model for business. Replace the central block (manager) with the term CEO and most of the other blocks remain the same. Those that change do so in terminology only; fans, for example, become shareholders.

In January 2001, the *Financial Times* carried an advertisement for the law firm White & Case. It showed a picture of Bill Shankly, legendary former Liverpool manager, striding in front of a packed Kop with his trademark Liverpool scarf around his neck and arms raised triumphantly. The tag line of the ad was: *One Person Can Make a Difference.* The text below the tag line confirmed the sentiment:

❝Bill Shankly was a man of conviction and an inspirational leader. As we continue to expand our corporate and finance practices, we need people with Bill's qualities. People who can push themselves and

inspire others … If you're looking for a chance to raise your game, get in touch.**99**

Is there a team or a business that doesn't want to raise its game? The modern football team, in its structure, orientation towards process and clearly defined performance criteria, is the model for modern businesses wishing to raise their game. The same is true for analysts and practitioners in information-rich and knowledge-dominated organizations.

Managers, like CEOs, set the tone, establish values and protect, or create, the culture; coaches, like functional managers, coach and develop the players so that they are able to implement the strategy established by the manager in a manner consistent with the culture; specialist coaches, like skills trainers, establish a level of technical expertise consistent with the implementation.

> In a football team, there are ultimately only two processes – scoring and stopping the opposition scoring.

In a football team, there are ultimately only two processes – scoring and stopping the opposition scoring. Coaches are gradually being recognized for their expertise in these distinct processes. For example, Don Howe, the former coach for the England national team, is considered to be a specialist in defensive play. Within each process, particular skills are required to execute the process designed by the functional coaches. It is the role of what the Americans call 'positional coaches' and what we call 'specialist coaches' to develop players' skills in order to deliver specific patterns of play. It is the role of the manager to select these coaches and players and then to motivate and support them.

This is another aspect of football management which has much to offer business. The manager does not sit, isolated, in a huge office which removes him from close contact with all levels of his staff. He is literally on the sidelines. However seldom he visits the training ground, his presence there changes the atmosphere and reinforces a level of contact. Most CEOs never attain such rapport. On match days the manager's contact is immediate and intimate. The duality of being 'the boss' and in the dressing room (workplace) provides great managerial strength.

However, it is a time balance which some managers, especially the new ones, find difficult to achieve. Brian Clough, one of the most successful managers in British football history, was notorious for his unpredictable and instinctive style of management. However, for all his eccentricity, he understood the demarcation of roles better than most. A story, possibly apocryphal, about Martin O'Neill, whose own managerial style owes much to the influence of his former manager, Brian Clough, reinforces the point. Apparently when O'Neill was at Wycombe Wanderers he mentioned to a player that he (O'Neill) had no idea how to play full-back. The player lamented: 'How can you coach me then?' 'I won't be coaching you,' came the reply, 'I'm too busy winning matches.' Be very sure, however, that coaching *is* happening at Celtic as it did at Wycombe and Leicester, where O'Neill was manager previously. As Graham Taylor, the former England manager, put it: 'Those who play off the cuff finish in the bottom half of the league.'

O'Neill will, of course, make sure that he selects the right senior management team to take care of the coaching side. However, he must not select them only for their technical ability – they must also fit the culture he has created, or wishes to create. It is what the great Liverpool teams of the Shankly/Paisley era called 'char-

acter'. Their motto was to assume a skill level and buy 'character'. By that, they meant someone who fitted the culture. Liverpool would drop players very quickly if it became apparent that the 'fit' did not exist. This sometimes happened despite exhaustive research into players' backgrounds. If they made a mistake, they cut their losses – another valuable lesson for business.

The value of coaching is, perhaps, the greatest lesson that business can learn from football. Too often, in business, coaching is mistaken for counselling or mentoring, to the detriment of the organization. While both functions are valuable to an organization and can be necessary sub-sets of coaching, genuine coaching is only about performance. In football, coaches are judged solely on performance. Nobody watches the process, only the results. Imagine the difference if business adopted the same appraisal system. Insert into an organization's appraisal system the concept of judging departmental managers solely on the performance of their staff. There would be no meetings between appraiser and appraised, only observation of the performance of staff. That is what happens on a daily basis with football teams. The entire management team is judged, each week, on what happens during each 90 minutes of competitive play. Kevin Keegan, former England manager and now manager of Manchester City, possibly an unlikely source, put the immediacy of judgement into perspective. He said: 'If you're Alex Ferguson, there are 70,000 people coming into your business for two hours on a Saturday afternoon and every week they publish a league table – businesses only have theirs published twice a year.'

It is the immediacy of such judgement, and the visibility of the managerial process, that makes football the all-embracing model it is. Where else are failures in personnel selection and man-management so totally visible? That visibility provides an access to

the process denied in business, at least until long after the event. As a consequence the lessons from the dugout are profound, not trivial. Whatever you think about football, an analysis of its management permits a profound understanding of the corporate managerial task.

WHAT TO EXPECT FROM THIS BOOK

Football, that is the core business itself, is the model which can provide lessons for managers at all levels of business. We have chosen to concentrate on high-profile managers who are generally considered to be the very best practitioners. A short biography of the greatest British managers is provided in Appendix A. We have chosen high-profile managers simply because of the accessibility to their working lives and their thoughts, as expressed in biographies, interviews and media reports. We could have chosen other less well-known managers to demonstrate best practice. There have been equally impressive managers at all levels of the game. Even at the semi-professional level there have been outstanding managers, such as the late Brian Hall, the first man to complete the non-league double with Wealdstone, or Geoff Chapple, whose FA Cup giant-killing exploits with Woking and Kingstonian are legendary. These men are equally valid models of managerial expertise. The manager of Dagenham and Redbridge, Garry Hill, was managing in the local Sunday league only three seasons before their magnificent 2001/02 season. When interviewed on TV he said that basically the processes were identical and that he expected the same to be true at any level. The same is true in business.

Another caveat we must place on record is the lack of accommodation for any gender issues. Football, at the highest level, is a male-dominated industry and as such, gender, as a managerial

issue, is not addressed in the book. We believe that this should not be a problem since the generic nature of the lessons provided by the game cuts across gender barriers. Indeed, it may also be that those with little interest in football, male and female alike, find the book useful in penetrating the murky world of sporting metaphorical analysis used by many business people when trying to explain complex managerial issues.

Finally, it is worth making the point that we have not attempted to highlight every single connection between football and business. The aim of the book is, primarily, to provide a detailed analysis of managerial best practice in a highly visible industry. Each reader can make many more links from their own experience than could ever be contained in a single book. However, we do not want to lose such insights and anyone interested in sharing their business/football connections can post them on the book's website at

Whatever you think of football, an analysis of its management enables a profound understanding of the corporate managerial task.

www.business-minds.com/goto/90minutemanager

PART II

The right man for the job

It is difficult to imagine any other industry effectively plucking someone from the shop floor to the chief executive office.

Fabio Capello (AS Roma)

The manager's background

WHEN ALEX FERGUSON ANNOUNCED HIS ORIGINAL INTENTION TO RETIRE AT the end of the 2001/02 season he provided Manchester United with a longer than usual period to select a successor. It also gave armchair selectors the opportunity to think about how best to choose Ferguson's successor. What type of manager, from what background, should replace him? Are there generic factors which not only Manchester United but all other organizations should bear in mind when searching for managers? What should they look for in a candidate's background before appointing that person to a managerial role? Should they look at his functional expertise and experience, that is the demonstrated ability to perform well at the job of managing others? Should the candidate have had training in how to manage? Should he necessarily be recruited from the same industry?

Anyone with experience in the workplace will have noted the seemingly arbitrary means by which people are frequently promoted to a management position. Looking at the experience of football can teach us a considerable amount about what to scrutinize most closely in a candidate's background.

INDUSTRY BACKGROUND

The first point to note is that there have been no instantly recallable instances in the modern era when someone who has never played football at any professional level has become a successful and well-known football manager. It is maybe surprising that successful managers in other sports have not been recruited to try their luck in football, given that managers with excellent track records are so rare and that the pressure to achieve success in football is so intense. This can be contrasted with business where, particularly at the top, professional managers do change industries. These include such heavyweights as Martin Taylor who left Courtaulds to head up Barclays Bank and Brendan O'Neill who left Guinness to take charge at ICI.

A common argument used against the idea of managerial interchangeability is that the players would not have sufficient respect for an individual who was asking them to do things which he had never attempted to do himself. However, it now seems increasingly acceptable in football to appoint a manager whose playing abilities were far inferior to those of the individuals in the team he is to manage. In other words, although football has not quite gone the whole way by appointing managers from outside the game, it is in fact gradually coming round to the conclusion that there is absolutely no link whatsoever between an individual's ability to play well and his ability to manage well. Gerard Houllier, who was only a semi-pro for a decade, famously said: 'You don't have to have been a horse to become a good jockey.'

> 'You don't have to have been a horse to become a good jockey.'

This would suggest there really is a managerial skill set which can be isolated, analyzed and, dare we say it, developed. That skill set would need to include 'street cred' which has always been a powerful indicator in football. However, the 'been there, done it' syndrome as a qualification for management, although still strong in football, is now becoming weaker.

FUNCTIONAL EXPERTISE AND MANAGERIAL ABILITY

We can point to several obvious examples in the modern era when a manager has successfully led a group of players who are far more skilled and talented than he could have even dreamed of being when he was a player. The playing and managerial records of Liverpool's Gerard Houllier, Arsenal's Arsene Wenger and England's Sven Goran Eriksson demonstrate the point precisely.

Gerard Houllier

Gerard Houllier started playing for little-known Le Touquet in France from 1973, when he was 26. Details of his playing career are not easy to discover, but his ability as a player was obviously limited for he started his career at a late age and then played only for a couple of years. Indeed, although he was studying for football coaching qualifications, much of his time in his twenties was spent completely outside football, teaching at various school levels, including some secondary teaching in Liverpool, before he became a lecturer in a high school of commerce.

His first appointment as manager was for Noeux Les Mines from 1976 to 1982, where he won promotion to Division Two in the French league. He became manager of Lens in 1982, earning the club qualification to the UEFA Cup, and won the French championship one year after taking over at Paris St Germain in 1985. Having displayed a considerable aptitude for management, he was drafted into the international scene in 1988, working first as assistant manager to the national team and then as manager in 1992–93. From 1990 to 1998, he was also technical director for the French Football Association. In 1998, his managerial abilities were recognized in England when he was appointed as joint manager of Liverpool (and, shortly afterwards, sole manager). In the 2000–01 season, his Liverpool side won three trophies.

Arsene Wenger

It is a sure bet that Arsene Wenger will be remembered for his managerial career rather than for his exploits as a player. He played for teams which are hardly major names on the international football circuit – few of even the most ardent football fans will have heard of Mulhouse, Mutzig or Vauban. He finished his career at Strasbourg and then as player/manager at Cannes. Like Gerard Houllier, he did not even devote himself fully to football until after his playing career was over. At the age of 25, during his time as a player, he obtained a degree in Economics from the University of Strasbourg.

In 1981, then in his early thirties, Wenger passed his coaching diploma and was appointed as Strasbourg's youth team coach. After a spell in charge at Nancy, he was appointed as manager of Monaco in 1987, where he won the French championship and made good progress in European competition. In 1995, he moved to Japan where in one season he transformed Grampus Eight from relegation contenders to runners-up and then cup winners. He was invited to manage Arsenal in 1996. At Arsenal he won the League and FA Cup double in 1998.

Sven Goran Eriksson

Sven Goran Eriksson is now the manager of the England team. The Football Association subjected themselves to much potential criticism for appointing a foreigner to lead the national side for the first time. However, they were prepared to withstand this criticism as they were sure that they were getting the right man for the job. That conclusion was based very much on Eriksson's attributes and experience as a manager. If they had taken his past playing abilities into account, it is fair to assume that Eriksson would have been overlooked for the post.

Eriksson enjoyed an undistinguished career as a semi-professional for Swedish second division side Karlskoga before injury forced his retirement at the age of 28. However, his managerial record since then has been outstanding. Appointed manager of Degerfors in 1976, he succeeded in promoting the club from the third to the first division in the Swedish league in three seasons. In two years at IFK Gothenburg, he won the domestic championship, two Swedish cups and the UEFA Cup. For Portugal's Benfica, he won three league titles and one cup. In spells at various major Italian clubs, he consistently achieved high placings in the league and won the cup four times. His period in Italy culminated in the winning of the league and cup double for Lazio in 2000.

Football teaches us from these three high-profile examples that having little functional ability does not preclude the possibility of going on to become an outstanding manager. But what about the other way round? Do great footballers make good managers? History tells us that they very rarely do. Let us look at a few examples.

GREAT PLAYERS TO GREAT MANAGERS?

Bobby Charlton is one of the all-time playing greats. He won several honours for Manchester United, captaining the 1968 team which won the European Cup. He was also a key member of the England side which won the World Cup in 1966. After his retirement in May 1973, he took over as manager of Preston North End. The team was relegated to the Third Division during his first season at the club and Charlton resigned from the post in August 1975. He never returned to management, apart from a spell as caretaker manager for Wigan Athletic in 1982–83.

Ask any English football enthusiast who the greatest goalkeeper has been in the past 30 years and the answer will more than likely

> What makes a player great has no bearing whatsoever on his potential as a manager.

be Peter Shilton. He won the European Cup twice with Nottingham Forest and was selected for a record number of appearances for the England national team. In March 1992, he took over as manager of Plymouth Argyle. The team was relegated at the end of that season. He was unable to achieve promotion in the following season and left the post in January 1995.

John Barnes and Chris Waddle were players who possessed the ability to excite audiences wherever they played. Generally recognized as two of the most exceptionally gifted players of their generation, they both represented England many times, often in the same team. Both have since tried their luck at management. In Waddle's one season in charge of Burnley in 1997/98, the team narrowly missed relegation to the Third Division and he left the post in May 1998. Barnes was appointed manager of Glasgow Celtic for the 1999/2000 season. By February 2000, Celtic had lost eight matches, were out of contention for the league and Barnes was fired.

Despite all the contrary evidence, there has been a lingering tendency in the past on the part of some clubs to think that a great player is more likely to make a good manager. The history of Leeds United is a classic case – they thrashed around unsuccessfully for years by appointing managers who had been outstanding players in the great Leeds team of the early 1970s, such as Allan Clarke, Eddie Gray and Billy Bremner. The club was even relegated to the Second Division before the board appointed Howard Wilkinson, a manager with little playing pedigree who went on to lead Leeds to the League Championship in 1992.

Although there have been instances where great players have gone on to achieve success as a manager – Franz Beckenbauer, Johan Cruyff and Kenny Dalglish are such examples – it seems obvious that what makes a player great has no bearing whatsoever on his potential as a manager. To be considered a great player, you do not need the intellectual ability to conceive of a long-term strategy, to be able to communicate effectively, to motivate others so that they realize their full potential. You simply need a high level of ability and a determination to succeed.

In fact, too much ability as a player can surely sometimes be a disadvantage when that person becomes a manager. If something comes naturally to a person, it can be difficult for them to convey how they do it to someone who does not possess such innate skill. Moreover, a talented individual can find someone with lesser ability frustrating to deal with. When the legendary Stanley Matthews eventually retired from football he had a short-lived job as manager of Port Vale, the club he had first played for. One player observed that when he was unable to perform a particular technique, Matthews would step in and demonstrate, perfectly, the required technique. 'That's what I want. Now you do it,' he would demand. He simply could not understand, nor empathize, with the plight of less talented individuals.

Steve McMahon, a player in the great Liverpool side of the late 1980s, has now managed Swindon and Blackpool, where the level of ability is bound not to be as high as the standard he was used to at Liverpool. This is an issue which McMahon is very much aware of. He says: 'The clubs where I played had high playing standards, so you've got to be careful not to judge everyone here by the standards I've been used to.'

NATIONALITY

If there have been no obvious cases of successful managers coming from outside football, there have been many where the manager has undergone his football education in another country. Arsene Wenger and Gerard Houllier are two such examples. Bobby Robson is an English manager who has won league championships in Portugal and Holland and a European trophy for Barcelona. Writing in 1994, the football journalist Hugh McIlvanney said that Alex Ferguson 'has already performed a major service by obliterating the claim that nobody could be a successful manager in England without coming up through the ranks of the English game'. Ferguson had played for and managed various Scottish clubs but did not experience English football until he was appointed manager of Manchester United in 1986.

The principles of good management thus appear to be universal. With a sound knowledge of the relevant industry, which can be learned, a proven manager is likely to find success in any environment in which he finds himself. Even the capacity to speak the native tongue fluently is not a prerequisite. It is hard to believe that Robson spoke Spanish or Portuguese entirely convincingly. In England, where foreigners not speaking the native language is much more of a rarity, the appointment as manager of Chelsea of Claudio Ranieri, an Italian who could not speak English, was met with disbelief in many quarters. Ranieri quietly confounded many of his early critics when Chelsea qualified for European competition in 2001. If Ranieri fails it will be because of a lack of managerial expertise, not because of his linguistic inadequacies.

CLASS

Many football writers have pointed to the working-class background of great football managers as a factor contributing to their success. They claim that the tight-knit mining (Shankly, Paisley, Busby, Stein, Robson) or ship-building (Ferguson) communities from which they hail have given them an appreciation of hard work, loyalty and solidarity among workmates.

This may be true, but it does not tell us much about the distin-guishing features of a successful manager. Football managers are almost exclusively ex-footballers, and footballers have traditionally come from working-class backgrounds. What is true about Shankly, Ferguson and the rest is therefore also true about countless managers who have made no impact whatsoever.

> Football managers are almost exclusively ex-footballers, and footballers have traditionally come from working-class backgrounds.

REGIONAL IDENTITY

What has not been mentioned but is actually quite a startling sta-tistic is how few managers born and brought up in the south of England have gone on to win the English league championship. Given the fact that the population living south of Birmingham forms the majority of the English population as a whole, it seems extremely odd that the last southern-born manager to win the Eng-lish league was Alf Ramsey with Ipswich in 1962. There have been several Scots in this period who have won it (Alex Ferguson, Bill Shankly, George Graham, Matt Busby, Kenny Dalglish), a French-man (Arsene Wenger) and a number of northern English (Harry Catterick, Joe Mercer, Brian Clough, Bob Paisley, Don Revie, Ron Saunders, Howard Kendall, Joe Fagan, Bertie Mee and Howard

Wilkinson), but no southerners. This incredible statistic may be explained to some extent by the greater popularity of football in the north of England and Scotland, but it still raises the politically incorrect possibility that the culture of some nationalities or regions is more likely than others to produce good managers.

PLAYING STYLE

As we discuss further in Chapter 3, a high level of enthusiasm and commitment, although necessary, is not sufficient by itself. Several players who on the pitch are seen as born leaders, vociferously cajoling others and displaying an intense hunger to succeed, are often deemed to be suitable material as potential managers. Terry Butcher and Bryan Robson are two such players who have failed to convince fully as managers.

Butcher was a fixture in the England team for several years in the 1980s and 1990s. On the football field, he was a picture of commitment. The abiding memory is of him sporting a bloodied bandage round his forehead as he played, a man literally bleeding for the cause of his team, coaxing those around him to even greater efforts. With such seemingly impeccable attributes as a leader, Butcher was an obvious choice to be appointed as manager by some club. He was duly approached by Coventry City in November 1990. His reign was not a happy one, however, and he was dismissed from the post in January 1992. Apart from a brief stint as manager of Sunderland in 1993, he has not returned to a management career on which such high hopes had rested. Bryan Robson was another outstanding player of the 1980s and early 1990s, captaining Manchester United and England during this period with great distinction. Nicknamed by the media as 'Captain Courageous', his intense will to win was always very evident. Appointed as manager by Middlesbrough in 1994, Robson has never fully won over his critics as manager. Despite spending liberally in the transfer market, it was literally an up and down period for him – promotion in 1995 and 1998 but relegation in 1997. Starting the season 2000/01 poorly, Middlesbrough appointed the experienced Terry Venables to take charge of first-team matters, with Robson forced to accept a more back-seat role. Robson finally left the club at the end of the season.

In contrast, laid-back players such as Terry Venables or George Graham have turned out to be thoughtful, demanding and successful managers. As the notoriously disciplinarian Graham himself said: 'I would never have picked myself as a player. I used to want to swan around, pass a ball here and there.'

It is easier to be a great motivator and leader when you do not have to make the necessary unpopular decisions incumbent on a manager. It is one thing being vociferously domineering on the pitch, but quite another to be coolly dispassionate in your appraisal of a situation and to be tough with those who do not accept your authority. Moreover, to be successful as a manager, leadership qualities need to be allied to other attributes such as strategic insight and vision. Analyzing the histories of the all-time great managers, it is fascinating to discover that many of them displayed a great interest in strategy and tactics even in their playing days. While their team-mates were just enjoying doing the job of playing football, managers such as Alf Ramsey, Bob Paisley and Jock Stein, while not necessarily outstanding players, were nevertheless thoughtful ones and spent much time contemplating structures and formations.

Jackie Milburn shared a room with Ramsey once when they played together for the English League side. He remembers how Ramsey talked half the night about tactics: 'Alf was never a great one for small talk when he was with England parties: football was

his one subject of conversation. He was always a pepper-and-salt man, working out moves and analyzing formations with the cruet on the table.'

Albert Stubbins has similar recollections of Bob Paisley, his team-mate at Liverpool:

&& Bob was not averse to having a discussion and to analyzing the game in the after-match bath. Most of us were just glad to get the mud off us and relax in the warm water. But if we'd conceded a goal we shouldn't have done, for example, he'd want to go into detail and try to work out how the other team had found a gap in our defence ... he was pretty accurate too. &&

Jock Stein was another great manager who from his early playing days was preoccupied more than his team-mates with the tactical intricacies of the game. His biographers Tom Campbell and David Potter describe Stein's playing career:

&& Every club he played for appointed him captain and allowed him to discuss tactics with the manager. He was also known as a thoughtful player, and to be frank, with his limited skill, he had to rely on cunning and knowledge of the game in order to survive. This meant that he understood more about the basics of the game than many of his more famous contemporary players who tended to play instinctively. &&

Businesses might, therefore, be advised to look for potential managers among those who profess an interest in and display a perceptive understanding of the running of the overall business.

More usually they turn to those office extroverts who display stereotypical leadership qualities of bravado and noise without the thoughtfulness necessary for real management.

However, while great on-the-field leaders may often not make great managers, they should not be discounted. If they are also thinkers about the game they are still likely to succeed. Peter Reid (Sunderland), Graeme Souness (Blackburn), Johan Cruyff, Franz Beckenbauer and Jack Charlton among others have all proved that on-the-field leaders can make the transition to management.

MANAGERIAL RECORD

The surest way of selecting the right manager to achieve a stated goal is by looking at their managerial record. The most reliable pointer to a manager's future success is whether he has achieved a similar goal in another organization.

When Manchester United were looking for a manager in 1986, Alex Ferguson was chosen because of his record in Scotland, where he had managed to break the long-time stranglehold of the Glasgow clubs with Aberdeen. He won the Scottish league three times, the Scottish Cup four times and a European trophy. This achievement made it more likely that he would be in turn able to break Liverpool's stranglehold in the English league in favour of United.

> The surest way of selecting the right manager to achieve a stated goal is by looking at their managerial record.

First, he had proven his ability to win trophies. Second, his period at Aberdeen had given Ferguson a great self-confidence that he could attain his goals. Success breeds success. As Ferguson says:

❝I am a winner. My whole life is about winning. Aberdeen gave me success and once you have sampled it, it gives you a background. You can then make use of the experience you have gained in becoming even more successful.**❞**

Moreover, a major factor contributing to Ferguson's success at Manchester United was that the board of directors gave him time (see Chapter 4), principally because they had substantial confidence in his abilities as a manager. That confidence was in turn due in large part to his record of achievement at Aberdeen. Past success thereby indirectly paved the way for future success.

Brian Clough won the League Championship for Derby County in 1972, a considerable achievement given the dominance of the large big-city clubs in the modern era. In January 1975, with the club struggling in the Second Division, Nottingham Forest rightly selected Clough as the man who could bring unprecedented success to a club of its size and history. What happened subsequently was surely the greatest managerial achievement in the history of English football. Within five years, the club had won the League Championship, the League Cup twice and the European Cup twice.

Glasgow Celtic were outperformed by their bitter rivals Rangers for most of the 1990s. In the 1999/2000 season, the club finished 21 points behind Rangers. Celtic turned to Martin O'Neill, the Leicester City manager, to change the club's fortunes. O'Neill's record in English football had been exemplary. He had taken Wycombe Wanderers from the non-league GM Vauxhall Conference to League Division Two and had won the FA Trophy twice. Leicester, a Division One club when he arrived, were promoted immediately under him and never finished below tenth in the Premiership. The team also qualified for three Worthington Cup

finals, winning two, and therefore qualified for European competition twice. His first season at Celtic was an unqualified success – the team won the league by a substantial margin and both domestic cups.

STRATEGIC FIT

O'Neill's appointment, however, constituted a major risk for Celtic. Ferguson and Clough had already achieved the category of success which the United and Forest boards were seeking. The Celtic board's goals would have been domestic dominance and significant progress in European competition. O'Neill's record within the context of the relatively limited goals of Wycombe and Leicester had been excellent, but he had never even attempted what Celtic were asking him to do. But there is always going to be an extremely limited number of available managers who have already achieved in the past what Celtic wanted in the future. Celtic therefore decided to take the calculated gamble of giving O'Neill, a successful manager at a lower level, a chance to see what he could do at a higher level.

This gamble has worked for Celtic so far, but there have been many instances in football when managers have been appointed to achieve a specific set of goals purely on the basis of their attainment of utterly different goals and have subsequently failed. Two examples of this are the experiences of Don Revie and Graham Taylor as managers of the English national team.

Revie took over as the England manager in 1974. He was appointed by the Football Association because of his outstanding success at Leeds United where he had won the league twice and the FA Cup and had achieved great consistency of performance from his team over a number of years. However, the time frame

he was allotted at Leeds to achieve his goals, the methods he used and the goals themselves were either irrelevant or unsuited to international football.

On his appointment as Leeds manager in 1961, Revie sought to build gradually the foundations of long-term success. He sought out young players with great potential. He built a tight bond of team spirit between the players. He had a close relationship with his team, willingly assuming the role of father figure by taking an interest in the players' personal lives and offering advice when necessary. The players responded with loyalty and commitment. Revie's influence at Leeds is summed up by one of his players of that era, Allan Clarke:

> **At club level, he was the best manager I ever played for. He did everything for us, fathered us, left nothing to chance. Anything we wanted, he'd do for us. He was that sort of guy. Right the way through the club they admired him. He got the utmost respect from everybody – the players, administrative staff and the commercial side. He was the gaffer.**

The England job was an entirely different challenge. To begin with, the demands were more immediate. At Leeds, it was three years after Revie's appointment before he won promotion to the First Division and eight years before he won his first League Championship. With England, his very first game in charge would have a bearing on achieving the necessary goal of progressing to the final stages of the European Championships. Failure to achieve this goal would result in a high level of condemnation from an impatient media and public which only eight years previously had witnessed an England team being crowned as World Champions.

There was no time in the few days of preparation for each international match for Revie to build a close relationship with his players or a profound team ethic among them. By necessity, managerial methods in international football have to be different. The manager has to select and organize a group of players with a high level of ability who play together rarely and might not even know each other particularly well on a personal level. The pool of available talent is fixed – it is impossible to recruit foreigners to play for your national team. On the pitch, the

> The pool of available talent is fixed – it is impossible to recruit foreigners to play for your national team.

players are generally pitted against another team of exceptionally gifted players. Tactical nous and short-term flexibility are thus much more significant attributes for an international manager than team building and long-term planning, Revie's real strengths. He duly failed to progress in the European Championships and was on the brink of failure to qualify for the 1978 World Cup when he escaped from the glare of public criticism by taking up a post as manager of the United Arab Emirates national team.

Graham Taylor's experience as England manager was similar to Revie's. His success at Watford, where he lifted the club from the Fourth Division to the First Division in the space of five years and then consolidated their new-found status, was also founded on finding and grooming young talent and on the careful fostering of a close-knit organization. This is how Taylor described his period at Watford:

❝What many people missed was that Watford FC was not just about a style of play or winning various divisions or cups. The Watford way was about the heart and soul of the club.❞

He added:

❝Here was a club in which players themselves became a family and the club and the town became very close-knit. This is how a football club could be a community. For a decade we saw the philosophy of a club and that was my achievement.❞

However, the qualities which earned Taylor success at Watford and in his other jobs at Lincoln City and Aston Villa were no guarantee to success as England manager when he was appointed in 1990. He failed when it mattered – the team did not progress beyond the initial stages of the 1992 European Championships and did not even qualify for the 1994 World Cup Finals.

Other managers, such as Kevin Keegan and even the great Alex Ferguson, to a certain extent have failed to make a successful transition from club to international football. Other managers have succeeded at a certain level of club football but not at a higher level.

Another example of the phenomenon of specialist managers is Joe Royle. Oldham Athletic's targets when he was appointed as the club manager in 1982 were presumably to consolidate the club's position in the Second Division and to do well from time to time in knock-out cup competitions. Royle actually exceeded these goals when he reached the final of the League Cup and the semi-final of the FA Cup in 1990 and won promotion to the First Division in 1991. His time in the top division with Oldham was

a struggle, however, with the team finishing in a low position in the league for two seasons before eventually being relegated in 1994.

Everton appointed him manager in 1994 on the strength of his achievements at Oldham. If he could exceed expectations at Oldham, surely he could do the same at Everton? However, this was an entirely different situation. The expectations were markedly higher. The Everton board and supporters believed that they should be challenging for the championship, as they often had throughout their history. Despite winning the FA Cup in 1995, Royle finished fifteenth and sixth in the league before resigning as the club contemplated the possibility of relegation in March 1997.

Another under-achieving large club, Manchester City, appointed Royle as manager in 1998. Despite suffering relegation soon after he took over, Royle achieved two promotions in successive seasons and City found themselves back in the Premiership amid claims from the media and supporters that the club was now back in the big time, ready to challenge the best. However, these hopes were dashed as City were relegated in their first season in the top division.

Royle's undoubted gift is to recruit players of a certain level of ability, motivate them and organize them into a cohesive unit. These were ideal attributes to succeed outside the top division and in one-off cup matches. To challenge for top honours over a full season in the Premiership, high-quality players and a more sophisticated tactical awareness and flexibility become necessary. In the case of Manchester City, Royle was too loyal to the players who had won the club promotion and the players he did recruit were not of a sufficiently high standard to give the team a chance of maintaining their status in the Premiership.

Royle was a perfect choice as manager when he was appointed, as City's goal was a return to the Premiership. However, once he had attained this particular goal, the club acquired a completely new goal – they now wanted to perform well in the top league. The strategic fit between the club's goals and the manager's proven abilities had ceased to look so right. Royle was sacked after City's relegation in May 2001 when, paradoxically, the fit had actually realigned itself (the goal now was once again promotion to the Premiership). A parting of the ways had come about a year too late for City.

Some football managers are more overtly recognized as specialists in a particular kind of situation. For instance, Dave Bassett and Barry Fry are seen as ideal to manage clubs which want to achieve the maximum possible on an extremely limited budget. In the 1990s, Ron Atkinson was recruited by Coventry City, Sheffield Wednesday and Nottingham Forest specifically to steady their respective ships which were in danger of sinking out of the Premiership. He succeeded with Coventry and Wednesday.

Turnaround management is a particular skill. Dave Bassett's appointment at Leicester City after Peter Taylor's dismissal shortly into the 2001/02 season was a result of the board's recognition of a short-term need (to stay in the Premier League). Bassett's remuneration package and contract reflected the task as designated by the board. Certain investment companies such as Jon Moulton's Alchemy group specialize in similar turnarounds – making a company viable for someone else to manage into the future. Bassett's appointment may be a classic example of a football Alchemy.

In business, there are also examples of individuals who have been seen to fit a particular type of strategic goal. A notable example of this is the great downsizer, 'Chainsaw' Al Dunlap, who famously turned round US companies Scott Paper and Crown-Zellerbach with his ruthless brand of management, before attempting the same at Sunbeam and eventually being fired.

CULTURAL FIT

Matching a future set of goals with a manager's record of achievement is therefore an important element in the recruitment process. It is also imperative that the culture, or corporate ethos, of the organization where the managerial candidate has previously established himself is not wholly at odds with that of the recruiting organization.

George Graham was the manager of Arsenal from 1986 to 1995. During this time, the club won the League Championship twice as well as the FA Cup. The keys to Graham's success at Arsenal were perceived to be discipline, organization, a keen work ethic and strong defence. The team was considered to be efficient rather than exciting and lacked what in football parlance is termed 'the flair player'.

Arsenal's rivals in North London are Tottenham Hotspur. Tottenham supporters pride themselves on possessing the completely opposite public image to that of Arsenal – while the team might not win trophies frequently, at least they are generally exciting to watch. After all, what is the purpose of football if the crowd is not entertained?

Graham's appointment as Tottenham manager in October 1998 was therefore not greeted with wholehearted enthusiasm. Although he won the League Cup in 1999, he never convinced the Tottenham faithful that he wanted to entertain as well as win. His relationship with the exciting winger David Ginola was a bench-

mark for Graham's relationship with the Spurs faithful. His antipathy towards Ginola was interpreted by the fans as an indication that he still prized efficiency and work ethic above any need to accommodate a flair player. He substituted Ginola no less than 17 times in one season and eventually sold him to another club. Graham was sacked in March 2001, despite having reached the semi-finals of the FA Cup, and was replaced by a former Tottenham flair player, Glenn Hoddle. Although Hoddle's record may not have been the best, his cultural fit most certainly was.

Manchester United have also long been known within the football world for placing a great emphasis on producing teams which play exciting, attacking football. This tradition has continued right through to the modern era. However, this capacity to excite also has a flip side. Whereas the great Liverpool teams of the 1970s and early 1980s were ruthlessly efficient, Ferguson's United frequently leave their victories to a breathless last minute or lose heroically, having committed themselves to a desperate, offensive onslaught. In 2000, in a vital match against European giants Real Madrid, United naively threw men forward in desperate search of a goal, only for their scant defences to be exploited by Real. After the match Ferguson almost proudly declared: 'That is the nature of this club.' This, in other words, is how United differentiate themselves. It is their corporate ethos – their brand.

Tommy Docherty, a United manager in the 1970s, was popular precisely because his view of how football should be played was consistent with this corporate ethos. His United team played with two attacking wingers, a rarity in modern football, including the flair player, Gordon Hill. Young, brash and skilful, although sometimes lacking in work rate, Hill was indulged by Docherty and loved by the supporters.

Docherty was sacked in 1977 after he was involved in a personal scandal. After the flamboyant Docherty, the board wanted a quiet life and opted for the thoughtful, intelligent Dave Sexton as manager. But Sexton's footballing philosophy was counter to the culture of the club. The emphasis switched from cavalier attack to structure and planning. Hill was deemed a liability and sold soon after Sexton's arrival. Neither his team nor Sexton himself exuded the passion characteristic of United in the past or indeed in the future under Ferguson.

Despite finishing second in the league in 1980 and winning the last seven games of the 1980/81 season, Sexton was sacked in the summer of 1981 and replaced by the larger-than-life Ron Atkinson.

> Certain events, such as being overtaken by Tesco if your name is Sainsbury, are unacceptable.

One of the inevitable consequences of a powerful brand is that failure to honour that brand can be a sacking offence. When Sven Goran Eriksson was finally moved on from Lazio he acknowledged that the demands of the brand were a significant factor. Eriksson explained: 'When you lose against Napoli at home, and the name of the club is Lazio, then nobody is happy.' Certain events, such as being overtaken by Tesco if your name is Sainsbury, are unacceptable.

MANAGEMENT TRAINING – IS IT NECESSARY?

The importance or otherwise of management training has become a major talking point in football over the past few years, just as it has in many other industries. Should a candidate have had a formal training in management before they can be consid-

ered for a post? Fabio Capello, the Roma manager, believes they should. His comments on the appointment of Gianluca Vialli to the Chelsea job in 1998 were unequivocal:

> ❝I don't know Vialli personally, or his abilities as a manager and a tactician. His situation at the moment is like driving a Formula One car without a licence. It's a situation that wouldn't be allowed to happen in Italy.❞

In the past, management training in British football was generally not even contemplated. Clubs would either recruit a manager with experience or a player at the end of his career seeking a management position. This state of affairs has been subjected to an increasing amount of scrutiny within the game. Howard Wilkinson, FA technical director and former manager of Leeds, raises typical objections to the traditional system:

> ❝I would love to play the concert piano. But I won't ever get a job with the Philharmonic because if I turned up they would say, 'Well, what have you done? Where have you been?' But in football, I can say, 'I want to be a manager' and I can get a job. Somebody will employ me just on the basis that I have said, 'I want to be a manager.'❞

He admits:

> ❝Given the high degree of special ability required, that's crazy. That's no good for anybody.❞

In many European countries outside Britain, obtaining a management post is impossible without the necessary education.

Gerard Houllier contrasts the British situation with the French experience, where management qualifications are mandatory:

66 Managing is a job you need to train for. But in England, anyone can manage a club tomorrow. Don, who is sweeping the floor, could be manager tomorrow if the chairman decided to put him at the head of the team. That couldn't happen in France. All the former players of our Golden Generation – Fernandez, Tigana and Giresse – worked hard to get their coaching education right. 99

Alex Ferguson stresses the need for practical on-the-job training before a player is appointed as a manager: 'I think that if people want to become managers, they should have some preparation. For example, working at a club for, say, a six-month period – not just management, but the coaching part as well as youth development.' Interestingly, Fabio Capello himself received his early management training in business. Capello went from playing into a management training position in one of Silvio Berlusconi's companies. From there he moved back into football with his first coaching job. This might be a useful model for any forward thinkers there might be in the football establishment to consider.

Going on management courses and learning from top managers on the job must undoubtedly be of considerable use. Some managers have surely benefited from learning from others. Several of the current top managers themselves played under highly successful managers for a considerable period of time. David O'Leary, the Leeds United manager, played under George Graham at Arsenal; George Burley, the Ipswich Town manager, played under Bobby Robson;

Martin O'Neill played under Brian Clough at Nottingham Forest; Glenn Hoddle played for Arsene Wenger at Monaco.

But what better management education can there have been than to witness either Matt Busby or Alf Ramsey at close quarters at work every day over several years? That was the real privilege for Bobby Charlton, and as we have seen, he did not stay long in management. What about playing for Matt Busby and being assistant manager to Alex Ferguson for several years? That seemingly unsurpassable management education did not help Brian Kidd. He left Ferguson, took on the manager's role at Blackburn but lasted less than a year before his team's poor form resulted in his dismissal. Learning from Revie did not help Allan Clarke, Eddie Gray or Billy Bremner as Leeds managers. Other examples abound and as George Graham points out: 'If being a good manager was as easy as just copying people, then all the people who played at Liverpool would be great managers.'

We have seen that it is prudent to match a candidate's past record with the specific future goals of the organization. That is certainly the safer bet. But a young manager has got to start somewhere. Matt Busby, Alf Ramsey and Don Revie were all appointed to their first management roles in their early to mid-thirties and built highly successful teams at their clubs within a few years.

So how should a recruitment panel react to a candidate who has no management experience? Or even more perplexing, to a young manager with a failure in management already to his name? Surely everyone deserves a second chance. (Bobby Robson and Alex Ferguson were both sacked early in their careers.) The key thing to look for in this situation is not training, although this should always be encouraged. Training – practical or academic, formal or otherwise – must always build on a crucial set of personality characteristics without which any manager would find it difficult to succeed.

Lesson

Look at their record, judge their strategic and cultural fit, check their managerial training – make your decision.

The manager's personality

LORD ALANBROOKE WAS CHIEF OF THE IMPERIAL GENERAL STAFF IN THE British Army during the Second World War. In his diaries he wrote:

> "Half our corps and divisional commanders are totally unfit for their appointments, and yet if I were to sack them I could find no better! They lack character, imagination, drive and power of leadership."

In a McKinsey survey in 2000, of the 6,500 senior and middle managers interviewed at 35 large US companies, 58 per cent said they had worked for an 'under-performer'. Of those 86 per cent said that working for an 'under-performer' made them want to leave the company. In a survey of US employee attitudes towards top management, workers were asked how their organization was managed – like a symphony orchestra, a medieval kingdom or a circus. Seventy-two per cent of workers chose either a kingdom or a circus. Nearly as many added that the leadership at their company was not inspiring.

Good leaders are hard to come by. Moreover, as the McKinsey survey confirms, poor management causes large-scale employee dissatisfaction. In 1999, Marcus Buckingham and Curt Coffman published a study which analyzed 25 years of Gallup interviews

with more than 1 million employees in a broad range of companies and countries. 'Talented employees need great managers' was their conclusion. 'The talented employee may join a company … but how long that employee stays and how productive he is while he is there is determined by his relationship with his immediate supervisor.' When they talk of managing people they are talking of a combination of what in football would be the manager's role and that of the coach – one responsible for direction and the other for implementation.

The promotion of people to their level of incompetence is a well-known phenomenon and nowhere more common than when players or coaches in football are asked to manage. Dave 'Harry' Bassett (Leicester City manager) said that in truth most managers would prefer to be coaches, out on the pitch working directly with the players. However, management is where the real money is, so that's where they are forced to go. The same is true in business. The money is in management. As a consequence, even though personnel may prefer to stay in a functional role, and that is where they can be of most value to the company, they are forced into management in order to climb the salary ladder.

Having a structure which pushes players into being managers when they have little aptitude for this role can have dangerous implications for a business. As we shall see, one of the key attributes of a top manager is the rare ability to be able to assess dispassionately other people's strengths and weaknesses. Poor managers are less likely to possess this ability and so are more likely themselves to select poor managers beneath them, thus perpetuating a potentially destructive cycle of employee dissatisfaction, with its resultant negative consequences for productivity and profits. The Work USA 2000 survey found that highly committed employees had a 112 per cent three-year return to

shareholders, compared with a 90 per cent return by those with average commitment and 76 per cent for low employee commitment. Although there has been no empirical research on this for footballers, we suspect the figures would be even more dramatic.

Yet despite the possible repercussions of the decision to select managers, how much effort and thought generally goes into the appointment of a first-time manager? 'Jim's a good salesman, he seems keen, let's make him manager of our sales team.' 'Helen's a good accountant, she gets on well with our clients, let's make her manager of our accountants.' But as we have seen in the previous chapter, there is no correlation between functional expertise and managerial ability. Functional expertise is also a lot more common. There are a lot more good sales people and accountants than there are sales people and accountants who would make good managers.

> There is no correlation between functional expertise and managerial ability.

Consequently, selections are made on a whole series of inappropriate, and mostly unspoken, criteria. Favouritism, fear of conflict or simply 'buggins' turn' dominate the selection process. If no real effort is made to seek those with genuine managerial potential or even to begin to assess what qualities might be inherent in a good manager, it is difficult to differentiate between a whole swathe of seemingly equally qualified candidates, all of them good sales people or accountants. The temptation in such a situation is to select the candidate you already know or like best or feel most comfortable with. At least then a senior manager can surround himself with a reassuringly friendly group of individu-

als, thus establishing a minor fiefdom or at higher levels a compliant power base within the company.

Such a policy would clearly be of little productive value to the organization. First, there is a good chance that the best potential managers have been overlooked (women and members of ethnic minorities can suffer especially from this clubby managerial environment). Second, other employees will feel excluded from what they perceive to be a self-serving management and self-perpetuating clique. Consequently, those employees become embittered and demotivated. The whole issue of selecting and running a management team is dealt with in detail in Chapter 6.

Another easy option is to select the candidate who seems the most keen or who shouts the loudest. These overtly assertive characters represent the stereotype cliché of a natural leader. But as we have seen in the previous chapter, the footballing equivalents of the office extrovert, the likes of Terry Butcher or Bryan Robson, do not necessarily make good managers. Moreover, two of the greatest managers of the modern era, Bob Paisley and Bertie Mee, did not even contemplate putting themselves forward for their first job as manager. Others identified their potential suitability for management – they looked past the current player and found the potential manager.

Bob Paisley, for example, talked of the time in 1974 when the Liverpool board approached him to offer him a promotion from assistant manager to being the great Bill Shankly's successor: 'I was quite content to go along as I was. The trainer's job would have seen me out. They had to talk me into it.' Bertie Mee was the club physiotherapist at Arsenal when he was offered the job as manager in 1966. He too was not exactly champing at the bit: 'It was a surprise but a very pleasant one. I had not planned to become a football manager. I was very happy in the career of my special interest, and I was enjoying a great deal of satisfaction from it. But I was urged to positions of responsibility.' The combined haul of Paisley and Mee in their first and only positions as manager was three European Cups, six League Championships and one League and FA Cup double.

We have analyzed the histories of several top football managers in order to provide some insight into the personality characteristics of the successful manager. There certainly seem to be several recurrent themes in their make-up. Most human beings will possess one or some of the following attributes. Football tells us that the talented manager will possess most of them. However, there is one characteristic without which no manager can survive and that is the desire to lead – in an environment that recognizes the need for a leader. Lawrie McMenemy, the manager who led Southampton to one of the biggest FA Cup final upsets when they defeated Manchester United in 1976, explains it in the following way:

66 Every organization needs a leader. The first thing you must do when you walk through the door is take charge. Then, every morning after that, look in the mirror and ask yourself: 'Do I want to be in charge?' If the answer is not an immediate yes, then get out. 99

OBSESSION

Jimmy Armfield was manager of Leeds United in the 1970s. Now a broadcaster, he explained why he never returned to football management after his resignation from Leeds in 1978:

66 It's a job for loners and that's not me. That's one of the aspects that took me out of the profession. You're often left with your own thoughts.

You can be sat watching the television at home, surrounded by family, and you don't see any of it. You're just thinking about what's going to happen in the next game. It does absorb everything else in life.**99**

He added:

66The real reason I left management was because it stopped me doing anything else and I felt that there must be other things in life. And I've found them.**99**

Jim McGregor was physiotherapist at several clubs, including Manchester United under Alex Ferguson, and was thus able to observe at close quarters the motivations and priorities of a manager:

66To be a successful football manager, unless you're unusual, you have to be totally committed to football. It is the most important thing in their life. A lot of their wives won't want to hear this, but I know from the managers that I've worked with that the game is their lifeblood. The wife unfortunately comes second, and I don't even think it's a close second in most cases.**99**

Alex Ferguson arrives at the club's training ground every week-day morning at 7.30 a.m. and he does not arrive home until after 9 p.m. Unless, of course, United play an evening match during the week. 'Sometimes', Ferguson says, 'if we have a night game away from home, I might not get home until 4 in the morning. But I just have half an hour's nap and then I'm up and out again.'

When United returned to Manchester late at night after a European Cup semi-final success in Italy, Ferguson went home to spend the night watching a recording of the whole of the other semi-final on television so that he could start to prepare for the final. He attributes his work ethic to his background: 'I know deep down that it has got to be the naturally hard-working background I come from. I am proud and happy to say that I had wonderful parents who worked hard and passed on to me the value of that ethic.'

Jock Stein's punishing work schedule was noted by John Rafferty, a journalist who followed Glasgow Celtic extensively during their successful period in the 1960s and 1970s: 'Stein worked extraordinary hours for the club ... In midweek when Celtic were not playing he would motor down (to Manchester, Liverpool or Leeds) after the afternoon's work was done at Celtic Park, talk a bit, watch the football, then motor back immediately afterwards and still be the first man at Celtic Park in the morning.'

Anyone who is prepared to work as hard as Ferguson and Stein must believe that the achievement of their work goals will afford them immense inner fulfilment and satisfaction and will signify their success as a human being. As Ferguson's career enters its final phase, however, he may be beginning to reassess his obsessive behaviour. He has said, for example:

> **As Ferguson's career enters its final phase, however, he may be beginning to reassess his obsessive behaviour.**

66 I missed out on seeing my children grow up. When I was at St Mirren I managed the club and two pubs and I would drop the kids off at school in the morning and I wouldn't be home until midnight. I did not see them grow up. 99

Many people would not place success in the workplace as a life priority. Many others would pretend that they do to colleagues and bosses, even to themselves, but in reality there will be limits to how much they actually do care. How many of us can claim the involvement and immersion in work similar to that of Herbert Chapman, manager of Huddersfield and Arsenal in the 1920s and 1930s, as described by a leading journalist of the time?

❝If you sat near him at a big match ... you realized the intense earnestness of the man. His face would go ashen grey as he lived every moment of the play. And when things were going against his men he seemed to be suffering mental agonies. I have never seen such concentration.❞

There is a story, told by a local team coach, about Bill Nicholson, the great Spurs double manager, that makes the point precisely: 'After Nicholson left the first team manager's job he remained on the Spurs staff in a youth development capacity. At around that same time I was in my very first coaching job as the coach of the youth team at Harlow Town. Quite innovatively at the time, Spurs sponsored the team and used it as a trialist staging post. Also, as the league allowed us to play two over-age players, Spurs could send convalescing players to us for a low-key rehab game. One horrible winter Tuesday night Bill Nicholson turned up to watch us play Letchworth Town Youth. So, there I am, sat next to the great man. Throughout the entire first half he did not stop talking (commentating and critically analyzing, to be more accurate). It was vaguely aimed at me, but realistically I imagined him doing the same if he were alone. At half time I asked if he'd like a drink. "No thanks," he replied, "the wife's waiting in the club house and we're going out for a meal, it's her birthday."'

One of the greatest managers, Brian Clough, was by no means a workaholic, although this does not mean that he was not obsessed. He took regular holidays through the season, and often the players would not see him at all in a working week until about ten minutes before the start of the game on Saturday. As Brian Glanville, the football journalist, said: 'He behaved very much like a pre-war manager – you didn't see him much and therefore when you did it was an occasion.'

Clough achieved phenomenal success as manager of Derby County and Nottingham Forest during the 1970s. However, after Forest won the European Cup in 1980, the team never reached the same heights again and was eventually relegated in 1993, the last year of Clough's management. This decline could be attributed to the fact that Clough relied almost exclusively on his undoubted talents as a motivator to bring him success. Unlike Alex Ferguson, Bill Shankly, Don Revie and others, he was arguably not prepared to put in the necessary day-to-day hard work to build the foundations for sustained dominance and consequently his success was more short term.

Steve Sutton, a Forest goalkeeper under Clough, described Forest's situation in 1993: 'The club needs to be shaken to the core. It has coasted in recent years.' Clough was no longer obsessed enough.

SWITCHING OFF

In an Institute of Management survey (Aldred, 2000), more than 70 per cent of UK business managers considered that work-related stress had adverse effects on their enjoyment of life, their home life, their health and their work effectiveness. This state of affairs is reflected in football. In 1996, Steve Coppell gave up the

job of managing Manchester City after only 33 days in charge, claiming that the struggle to revive the struggling club was making him ill:

❝ I'm not ashamed to admit that I have suffered for some time from the huge pressure I have imposed on myself and since my appointment this has completely overwhelmed me to such an extent that I cannot function in the way I would have liked to.❞

In 1991, Kenny Dalglish resigned from Liverpool, citing the personal pressures resulting from the crowd disasters at Heysel and Hillsborough. Five years later, Dalglish again turned his back on the stress of football management, this time at Blackburn.

The stress experienced by other managers has adversely affected their performance and consequently that of their team. According to many football commentators, Don Revie, Bobby Robson and Kevin Keegan have all been managers who have betrayed anxieties which transmitted to the players and were therefore detrimental to their teams' success.

Despite Leeds' pre-eminence during the 1960s and early 1970s, Revie's team won the League just twice, finishing second five times. Robson has said that his 'one regret was not winning a championship with Ipswich. 'On three occasions I felt we were the best team in the League but we couldn't win it.' Johnny Rogan, in his book *The Football Managers*, likened Robson to Revie:

❝ Both managers betrayed considerable tension in the dug-out and their teams seldom received their just deserts in cabinet silver. Like Leeds, Ipswich often gave the impression that even if a trophy was presented to them they might still find some way of losing it. Their late

season fatigue was mirrored in the visage of their harried, overworked manager. 99

Kevin Keegan's Newcastle team was several points ahead of Manchester United towards the end of the 1995/96 season. As the manager began to show increasing signs of stress, the team's form faltered considerably, losing four of their last eleven games and eventually losing the title to United. Keegan's tension eventually boiled over in the now infamous television interview after one of the final games of the season. He reacted to Alex Ferguson's perceived provocations by launching into a finger-jabbing tirade against his rival. Keegan's reputation has never entirely recovered. The perception that he reacts badly to stress and has an inclination to walk creates an image of psychological fragility not conducive to top management.

> As the manager began to show increasing signs of stress, the team's form faltered considerably.

Even Ferguson himself, early in his United career, seemed to be weighed down by the immense pressure of trying to win the championship for the club for the first time in a generation. Indeed, in the 1991/92 season, just as it seemed that United were about to break this sorry sequence, United's form collapsed and they won only three of their last eleven games, thus losing out to Leeds. Many blamed the manager's clearly visible tension for this demise. Ferguson, despite his still evident passion and commitment, cuts a more relaxed figure these days. He attributes this development to a newly found ability to relax: 'I have found a way of switching off now. You have to do that. It is the only way to survive. I am now able to withdraw and give myself thinking time.'

In recent years Ferguson has found release in horse-racing:

> It's been a good release for me. It's helped me to keep going. After a game you're tired, especially after one of the big European games. You can imagine the emotion that goes into them. I can get the first flight down in the morning and be on the gallops at Newmarket at 8 a.m. I am back in the afternoon, fresh.

Arsene Wenger handles stress similarly: 'When I'm about to lose it, I get away, do something else and come back a different man. That's experience.'

However, even such distraction cannot overcome the physical and mental exhaustion which many years in charge exerts on managers. Ferguson admits the pressure is getting to him:

> There is always a headline that judges you, whether you are innocent or guilty. It is very difficult to live like this. Eventually it wears you down. Remember, I have been doing this now for 15 years at United alone.

An inability to handle stress reduces a manager's effectiveness and inevitably communicates itself to the team, creating a negative impact on their performance. However, given that managers view their job as a life priority and, as a consequence, are totally committed, the search for psychological stability is hard. Perhaps a dose of the following philosophy from Peter Reid, the Sunderland manager, would do all managers some good:

> You can never get away from football, but the only thing they can do is sack me, and worse things happen at sea.

As Gerard Houllier's heart surgery highlighted, football can be hazardous to your health. Like corporate CEOs, football managers lead a highly stressful and generally unhealthy lifestyle. Constant travelling, long hours, virtually permanent pressure and continual socializing, with all that entails, are guaranteed to place the body and mind under enormous strain. Graeme Souness had a triple bypass, while Johan Cruyff also had open heart surgery; Joe Kinnear (then manager of Wimbledon) was also extremely ill and Jock Stein actually died in the dug-out during one of Scotland's World Cup qualifying games. However, those who survive cannot turn their backs on the game they love. This is where obsession comes back into the equation. Arsene Wenger explains the problem very clearly:

66Your health should always come first. Unfortunately for most managers, passion for the game comes first most of the time. The pressure is there and you have to cope with it. You can't forget about it, especially if you play every three or four days. You have the next game in your mind straightaway.99

An article in the December 2000/January 2001 *Harvard Business Review* (Loehr and Schwartz, 2001) argues that the only way to deal with the stresses imposed on CEOs is for them to treat their work schedules as athletes would treat theirs. The authors have worked extensively with sports people and assert that in order to perform at the highest levels, over an extended period, senior managers must 'train in the systematic, multi-level way that athletes do'. Perhaps the most important issue the authors expose is the need to develop what they call a personal Ideal Performance State (IPS). While managers 'can perform successfully even if they smoke, drink and weigh too much ... they cannot perform to their full potential or without a cost over time'. In order to

develop their IPS they must begin to understand the need to be able to 'mobilize energy on demand'.

Surprisingly, their research shows that 'the real enemy of high performance is not stress, which, paradoxically as it may seem, is actually the stimulus for growth. Rather the problem is the absence of disciplined, intermittent recovery.' The research merely confirms the common-sense understanding that you need to balance energy output with energy replenishment. In the case of CEOs and football managers this means both physical and mental energy levels. Naturally, individuals must establish the correct balance for themselves. Those who fail to do so are a danger to themselves and to their businesses.

ANALYTICAL SKILLS

A manager can be a complete obsessive and work as hard as he likes but he will not make sustainable impact unless there is an intelligent structure and focused direction to his work. A good educational record is normally perceived as a reliable indicator that a person possesses an analytical mind. Football managers are generally ex-footballers who have dedicated themselves to the game from a very early age and are, therefore, mostly lacking in formal education (Arsene Wenger and Gerard Houllier are obvious exceptions).

> The great managers clearly have a highly developed intelligence.

However, the great managers clearly have highly developed football intelligence. They have an intuitive analytical ability, whether they had a formal education or not. As we will discuss in Chapter 5, building the foundations for sustained success requires a thorough examination of every last detail of the running of the club and reaching a profound sense of what exactly must be done to achieve the established goals. Undertaking this task at an organization as large as a major football club is surely a considerable intellectual exercise. The manner in which the great managers perform this exercise testifies to their analytical capabilities.

The transparent demonstration of analytical prowess also augments a manager's authority which must, in turn, enhance the performance of the team. If the team has confidence in the manager, they can focus on performing well, without worrying that doing so will have little effect because the overall strategy is wrong. As Bobby Charlton said of Matt Busby: 'You always knew that he knew more than you did, and if ever you thought to yourself, I wonder why he doesn't do so and so, you'd find that a few days later it had happened.' The confidence the players had in Busby enabled them to attempt tasks they may have considered beyond them. Why? 'Because the boss said we can do it.'

The difference between the reactions of players and media to the last two England managers, Kevin Keegan and Sven Goran Eriksson, highlights this issue very well. Keegan's strengths were not perceived to be analytical ability or judgement but rather an infectious enthusiasm and motivational ability. When managing the national side, he persisted with playing a 4–4–2 playing formation (that is, four defenders, four midfielders and two strikers). The media in particular did not like this, thinking the system old-fashioned and unsuited to the more sophisticated demands of international football. After England's early exit from the European Championship finals in 2000, a comment by one of the players, Martin Keown, led people to suspect that even the players had little confidence in Keegan's tactical judgement. A couple of days

after England were eliminated, he said: 'The bottom line is that we were inept tactically and we were exposed against teams we could have beaten.' This lack of confidence in the manager's analytical ability must surely have had a detrimental effect on the team's performance.

In contrast to Keegan, Sven Goran Eriksson projects an image of quiet authority. He is portrayed as an intelligent and studious individual. He has also employed the 4–4–2 system in every game for England to date. There has barely been a murmur of protest, even from the media. If Eriksson does it, it must be right.

GETTING THINGS DONE

When asked what drives him, Alex Ferguson replied: 'I call it the last-minute syndrome. The build-up to the final whistle creates this incredible excitement and tension, then after about an hour it's gone. It's recreating that last-minute feeling.'

A manager can work hard conceiving and planning a well thought-out long-term strategy, but unless he is prepared to oversee its efficient implementation, the exercise will remain purely academic. In a 1999 *Fortune* magazine study of business management failure (Charan, 1999), poor implementation is blamed for approximately 70 per cent of the cases analyzed. As the author puts it:

> ❝In the majority of cases ... the real problem isn't the high concept boners the boffins love to talk about. It's bad execution. As simple as that: not getting things done, being indecisive, not delivering on commitments.❞

It is clear in Chapter 5 how managers who seek to establish the fundamentals for sustained success have possessed an almost

pedantic concern with every last detail of the running of the club. They may delegate well (see Chapter 6) but their constant realization of the need to get things done ensures that they remain involved in the day-to-day workings of all areas of the club and this keeps them in touch with all aspects of the operation. This operational sensitivity is one of the key lessons that football management provides for business. It is too common for CEOs to claim that they are too busy to maintain such contact with the operational element of huge corporations. The *Fortune* survey shows that if they do not, they will fail. It may be difficult but it must be done.

ATTENTION TO DETAIL

However, the mere desire to get things done is not sufficient in itself. Without an organized mind, an eye for detail and an excellent memory, the manager will not be able to retain a grasp of the complexities of all the various areas of the organization and will not, therefore, be able to judge where or how to act. Indeed, a phenomenal memory is attributed to several of the great football managers. Tom Saunders, a member of the Liverpool management team during their period of dominance, said of Bob Paisley:

❝Every scrap of information is stored in his memory. He astounds me by recalling really detailed incidents of matches we saw a long time ago ... After we've watched a weekend match together, often he'll hardly say a word for long periods on the journey home. That's probably when he's concentrating and reflecting on what he's seen at the game, which he can instantly recall.❞

Eric Harrison, responsible for youth development under Alex Ferguson, has similar observations about the United manager:

"He has a photographic memory. He'll name you the team that played Charlton three years ago and be 99 per cent right. I think, also, he plans his games from the start of the season. I've never asked him, but I think he looks at the fixtures and does a lot of forward planning.**"**

Football is so obviously a people industry that the recollection of personal contacts and details is a primary managerial skill. The ability to 'know' the right people is central to all the great managers at every level. Being in the same room as Dave 'Harry' Bassett (Leicester City), Stan Ternant (Burnley) or Barry Fry (Peterborough), for example, provides a master class in networking. There appears to be no one they do not know or who does not know them. Knowing who you can turn to is a key attribute. George Bush Snr, for example, was known as the 'Rolodex' president because his simple card index had everybody's name in it – not least because one of his previous jobs had been as head of the CIA.

> The ability to 'know' the right people is central to all the great managers at every level.

Football managers, like chief executives of large organizations, come into contact with innumerable people in their working lives. Matt Busby did not seem to have any trouble remembering all their names. Paddy Crerand, a United player under Busby, recalls the time when he briefly introduced his friend Jim Daly to the manager before a game. Months later, just after United had won a cup final, Busby spotted Daly in a crowd, walked over and asked, 'Well, how are you, Jim?' The best CEOs and heads of large departments are the same. They

make it a matter of pride that they know their workforce well. Even if it is difficult to remember names and faces there are tricks and mechanisms for providing the illusion. It is worth making the effort to learn these in order to at least create the impression of empathy – although obviously genuine empathy is even more powerful.

An ability to see the big picture and a keen eye for detail are often seen as two conflicting, maybe even mutually exclusive, human qualities. Football tells us that the best managers possess both.

DRIVING AMBITION

Robert Browning's observation that 'a man's reach should exceed his grasp; else what's a heaven for?' could be the guiding principle for all great managers. The Liverpool goalkeeper of the time, Ray Clemence, recalls an episode on the team coach shortly after the club had first won the European Cup, in 1977:

❝Bob (Paisley) overheard Steve Heighway saying the 1977 team should have an annual reunion because the Rome win had been so special. Bob went absolutely bananas. 'Never mind bloody reunions. We've got to look forward to winning something this year, next year and the year after that.'❞

Liverpool went on to win Europe's premier competition three more times in the years up to 1984. Similarly, Ferguson has spoken of the desire to continue to achieve:

❝Winning a trophy doesn't really mean anything to me when it's gone. At the time it's the most important thing. But as soon as it's over, it's soon forgotten. The next step is the important one.❞

If a manager's ambition is easily satisfied by a short burst of achievement, he will not have the drive to ensure continued success. Another possible explanation for the decline of Brian Clough's management powers is that his success in the 1970s sated his hunger for success, thereby blunting his ambition. The test of true greatness is never to win the championship once. The football or business equivalents of the pop world's 'one-hit wonders' can never claim greatness.

Liverpool's sustained success over a period of two decades was due in large part to the corporate culture of unceasing ambition instilled by Bob Paisley and before him by Bill Shankly. Peter Thompson, who played in Shankly's team, says: 'When we won the cup (in 1965), he (Shankly) went to bed that night and said that he was planning the next few seasons. He could never stop and celebrate.'

Over the past few years Manchester United have been the only other English club in the modern era to achieve a comparable period of sustained dominance in the domestic league. Again, it is the manager, Alex Ferguson, despite having won so much in his career and now 60 years of age, who possesses the permanent desire to win which imbues the whole atmosphere of the club and enables success to be maintained. As Peter Schmeichel, the United goalkeeper for much of the Ferguson era, has said: 'He wants to win every game he takes part in and he puts that over to the players. He is the driving force. He still has the hunger.'

The United manager's continuing hectic daily schedule testifies to this. Ferguson himself says: 'Being successful doesn't mean you can forget about work ethics, doing your homework or focusing on the basics of your job.' Notwithstanding other criticisms levelled at him, Microsoft founder Bill Gates is driven by insatiable ambition. Clearly money does not drive Gates. The need to

be viewed as the greatest is what fuels him and his players. The sight of Steve Bullmer, CEO of Microsoft, jumping around the stage and punching the air at an AGM may amuse many, but it motivates his team and demonstrates his commitment in a very real way. Similarly, Richard Branson's undoubted ambition rubs off on his staff at Virgin.

UNBRIDLED ENTHUSIASM

Meredith Belbin, the management theorist, researched the distinguishing features of chairmen of successful companies and found that they tended to be 'naturally enthusiastic with that extrovert capacity for excitement that is known to motivate others' (Belbin, 1981). This theory is only too obvious in football. The best managers love their work. This makes working so hard rewarding rather than burdensome and serves to enthuse those around them.

Anecdotal evidence emerging from the England dressing room suggests that not only is Sven Goran Eriksson an immensely confident manager with a meticulous, almost scientific approach to the game, he also has a superb work ethic. Players (and workers) respect the work ethic in their bosses. The view that the manager is as dedicated, hard-working and competent in his job as he is asking you to be in yours is a powerful managerial tool. Eriksson demonstrated this work ethic even before he had met the players. He and/or his assistant Tord Grip went to a Premiership game at virtually every opportunity from the day of their appointment until their first full meeting with the team.

> Players (and workers) respect the work ethic in their bosses.

Tommy Smith, the former Liverpool player, reminisces about Bill Shankly's natural enthusiasm for the game: 'Say you went in during the morning and said, "Good morning, boss." "Aye, son, good day for football." And if it was raining, "Aye son, good day for skidding the ball." Everything was associated with football.' Earlier on in Shankly's career, soon after he had been appointed as manager of Huddersfield, a local journalist wrote: 'The new appointment has been a popular one with the players. Mr Shankly has aptly demonstrated an abundant enthusiasm and perhaps, more important, a remarkable capacity for passing on his enthusiasm to those under his supervision.'

Marcello Lippi, the renowned Italian coach, remembers vividly seeing a television clip of Alex Ferguson dancing around on the touchline after a United goal: 'In that moment I had a glimpse of what makes him tick. Here was a man so passionate about the game and obsessed with winning. I am sure he passes on those characteristics to his team.'

Ferguson himself says:

❝Management is a fascinating subject. I hear and read different descriptions about what makes a top manager. Great coaching, intelligence, decision making, so many things. But too often we overlook the basic factor, which is enthusiasm. It's vital to have that. Desire and enthusiasm rub off on other people.**❞**

Kevin Keegan might lack tactical nous but his almost childlike enthusiasm is legendary in the football world. Steve Howey played for Keegan at Newcastle and now plays for him again at Manchester City. He says of him: 'It's impossible to dislike Kevin. You came in one morning feeling down but watching him whizz

about brought you back to life. He wasn't really bothered about things like practising free kicks but he made five-a-side feel like the World Cup.'

When the manager loses enthusiasm, the team suffers. Gerard Houllier recognized this when he began feeling unwell prior to his illness in late 2001.

> ❝I love my job but during August and September I was feeling reluctant to go to work. Physically, I felt something was wrong, but I did not show it to my players. If you show you are weak, the team will be weak.❞

Whether you call it passion or obsession, the total commitment of great managers provides a model of the work ethic they demand of their workforce. A comment from a colleague of the film director Stanley Kubrick demonstrates that such commitment is a general managerial characteristic. He said:

> ❝Everybody earned their pay when they worked with Stanley, but nobody earned it as much as Stanley. There was nothing in life for Stanley outside of the film.❞

POSITIVE DISPOSITION

Alex Ferguson's favourite quotation is said to come from Vince Lombardi, the great American football coach: 'We never lose, we just run out of time.' In his survey, Belbin (1981) states that another feature of successful company heads is that they think in very positive terms and rarely use negative terminology. Any defeat hurts, but the great manager will not allow it to diminish his ambition for the future and will emerge from it even more determined.

Don Revie's Leeds team was humbled by second division Sunderland in the 1973 FA Cup Final in what has gone down in football folklore as one of the greatest shock results in history. Minutes after the final whistle, Revie warned his players: 'I'll make you sweat blood.' One of the players, Allan Clarke, recalls that 'we did sweat blood. There was no limit to his ambition'. Leeds won the League Championship in 1974.

Hugh McIlvanney remembers meeting Jock Stein the morning after Celtic were knocked out of the European Cup in 1969:

> ❝It was like entering a bereaved household and the only possible reactions were sympathy and an embarrassed search for the right thing to say. Jock Stein, the head of the house, was there dispensing condolences and reassurance. Immaculately suited, his face shaved and polished to an optimistic shine, he came forward with a smile that was even broader than usual, a handshake that was even firmer.❞

Celtic reached the European Cup Final the following year.

Brian Clough's managerial style was certainly coloured by his natural optimism and his desire to emphasize the positive. The experience of John Robertson (now Martin O'Neill's right-hand man at Celtic) was a classic example:

> ❝When Brian Clough first came into Nottingham Forest, everyone at that time picked on all the things that I couldn't do, as far as football was concerned – I couldn't tackle, I couldn't head, I wasn't the quickest person – but it didn't seem to worry him at all and he concentrated on things that I was good at.❞

He explained:

> **❝** He was the one who moved me from midfield to left wing, and from then on I went from strength to strength, because he knew that I could go past people, he knew the final product was good and he was more positive, rather than worrying about the things I couldn't do. **❞**

Clough's positive nature is further demonstrated by player recollections of his team talks. At half-time during a match, discussion centred around what was to come rather than a post-mortem of mistakes in the first half. If his team lost, Clough did not criticize the players in the dressing room. Alan Durban, formerly of Derby, says: 'Clough was very good at either disappearing or picking us up. He wasn't one to wallow in self-pity.'

> If his team lost, Clough did not criticize the players in the dressing room.

Surely one of the greatest examples of the triumph of will over circumstance is the career history of Matt Busby. Most of the young United team which Busby had painstakingly nurtured were killed in an air crash in 1958. Despite being seriously injured himself in the crash and being devastated by the tragic loss of young men under his management, Busby was persuaded to continue and went on to build another great team which eventually won the European Cup in 1968.

HUNGER TO LEARN

Herbert Chapman was no snob when it came to receiving ideas which might help him improve the way he did his job: 'I would

borrow one from a programme boy at Highbury if it were a good one.' Jock Stein's thirst for knowledge and new ideas was described by Jimmy Farrell, a director at Celtic throughout Stein's reign: 'He was always asking questions … he wanted information about things.' In 1963, while still manager of Dunfermline, Stein went to Italy to witness at first hand the training methods of the highly respected Inter Milan coach Helenio Herrera. When he returned, Stein experimented with the new tactical strategies he had witnessed, with considerable success.

Similarly, Alex Ferguson sent his assistant Brian Kidd to witness various European clubs' training methods so that best practice could be assessed and then replicated at Manchester United. Stan Cullis, the great Wolverhampton Wanderers manager, made several trips behind the Iron Curtain during the 1950s to study the methods of the Russians and Hungarians, who were then at the forefront of tactical thinking.

George Graham reads as much as he can about those managers he respects. 'The managers I admire abroad are Giovanni Trappatoni, Arrigo Sacchi and Louis van Gaal. I admire people who have won things. I like to read their autobiographies to see what makes them tick.'

Not only should managers always be open to new ideas, they also need to adapt quickly to a changing or even completely different environment. This is something which Brian Clough uncharacteristically failed to do in his short spell at Leeds United in 1974, as we will see later. He attempted to employ the same dictatorial motivational tactics he had used selectively in the past and was effectively forced out of his job by the established Leeds star players who were not accustomed to being treated in this way.

It is interesting to note that Clough was replaced by the self-effacing Jimmy Armfield. Within 12 months Armfield had very quietly removed the core of the resistant players. By using a far less confrontational style Armfield had produced the desired effects. Armfield had, perhaps, learned from Clough's mistakes. Another lesson from the Clough/Leeds story is to be careful who you 'bad mouth'. While at his previous club, Derby County, Clough had consistently criticized the attitude, ethics and methods of the Leeds players, little knowing that one day he would rely on those same players for his job.

Even when a manager has been in the game for many years, albeit in another capacity, that desire to learn remains crucial. Bob Paisley admitted that the first year of management was a steep learning curve for him after so many years as assistant to Bill Shankly. But he was quick to heed the necessary lessons: 'It's taught me that I've got to make decisions that may not be popular with everybody. I've learned to be more relaxed and realized that some jobs can be done in one hour instead of sweating on them for days.'

Alex Ferguson believes he has gradually learned how to become a better manager over the years: 'I became obsessive more or less, but you get to a peak where the obsession is no use. It's energy using up energy. When you mature you start observing more and that's when you become a better manager.' In the past, Ferguson admits he may have been too hard with players. 'But it suited the environment I was in at the time, at St Mirren and Aberdeen. Coming to Manchester United I carried on a bit of Aberdeen for a spell. But then I needed to start thinking – this was different, this was expectation, this was big league, this is the biggest.'

SELF-BELIEF

We have already mentioned two fine balances which the manager must seek to strike – being committed to work but being able to switch off and being able to see both the big picture and the small detail. The best managers also balance flexibility and decisiveness. New ideas have to be entertained, but a manager cannot be swayed by every opinion. He must have the self-confidence to accept some viewpoints but reject others which he does not share.

We can take the histories of two England managers to demonstrate this point. England managers are in particular need of a large dose of self-belief in their decision making as they are always under immense pressure from the media and public, especially as far as selection of the team is concerned. Everyone has their own idea of who should be in the national team and managers will always be criticized for persevering with certain players or for ignoring in-form players whose style of play makes them popular with the public.

> The best managers also balance flexibility and decisiveness.

Alf Ramsey was not a man afraid to make difficult decisions. The best example of this was during the 1966 World Cup when he ignored a media clamour for the great goalscorer and popular hero Jimmy Greaves to be reinstated for the final in favour of Geoff Hurst, a youngster with little international experience. Despite his undoubted talents, Ramsey did not believe Greaves fitted into the team structure as well as Hurst. Hurst scored in the quarterfinal and his famous hat trick in the final won the World Cup for England.

Don Revie, on the other hand, did not seem to have the same inner belief in an overall plan when he was England manager and was thus vulnerable to constant press demands to amend his tactics and introduce the players of the moment. A classic example

of this was when he picked Stan Bowles for a vital World Cup qualifying game in 1976. Bowles was popular with the public, but he was precisely the type of talented individualist whom Revie had shunned in his days at Leeds when he had instead concentrated very much on the team ethic. Ted Croker, then Secretary of the Football Association, believed that Revie did not have the necessary will to assert his own ideas:

&& As far as the team goes, I honestly don't think he ever picked the team he wanted. It was what the press said. For instance, he picked Stan Bowles to play in Italy for what was probably the biggest game of his managerial career ... For Revie, picking him was against the grain. It wasn't Don Revie. He seemed to be doing things he wasn't sure about. 99

He added:

&& He was gambling, though he didn't know when he was gambling, doing what the press wanted and hoping it would come right. It got to a stage when people were saying that you'd soon be able to buy England caps from Woolworths. 99

Alex Ferguson describes how he has forced himself to stick to his basic principles:

&& I said to myself that if I'm going to survive, I'm going to have to be quite firm. In other words, I would not change my principles and if you don't like it – goodbye. I've tried to keep these disciplines ... I probably made a conscious decision to make sure I was hard enough to survive. 99

The necessary self-belief which the best managers have means, however, that they will not always bow to authority. Indeed, they tend to have a rebellious, outspoken streak. Ferguson has always had an uneasy relationship with the United board. When Bob Kelly, the then Celtic chairman, told his board about Jock Stein, he said: 'I think I've found a manager, but he'll make life hard for us.' Tony Balfe, the Grantham chairman, remembers interviewing Martin O'Neill for his first managerial post: 'He was the sort of man who looked you in the eye and wanted answers. He interviewed me as much as I interviewed him.' O'Neill's ruthless insistence on the removal of any vestiges of the Dalglish regime at Celtic merely confirms Balfe's judgement.

PEOPLE SKILLS

There is a popular misperception in management and business literature. It is that there are so-called 'people' businesses which are in some way unique. The reality is that *all* businesses are people businesses. Admittedly, there is now a greater awareness of the value of human capital to the bottom line than in previous eras, but the need to handle people has always been crucial to organizational success. An intuitive understanding of what makes others tick is, therefore, a key characteristic of good management. The fashionable attempts to codify this intuition in work such as that on emotional intelligence (EI) generated by Daniel Goleman's 1995 book of the same name cannot provide methods of attaining the skills, it only provides ways of recognizing it. The truth is that we do not need books to recognize it, we actually recognize it the moment we see it. The ability to be able to connect with people is obvious, intangible and essential.

A developed awareness of others is perhaps the most important feature of a manager's make-up in any business. First, it enables them to select the most suitable candidates for recruitment after the inevitably superficial interview process. Second, it will enable them to identify quickly the strengths and weaknesses of those who work for them and assess their potential. In this respect, people intuition in business is more difficult and, therefore, even more important than in football. On a football pitch, it is more obvious which people have ability than in a large company or department, where disguising or hiding failings and lack of commitment can be a popular employee pastime. In the corporate world, perception can easily be allowed to preside over reality. Third, any attempt at motivating others will generally fail without an advanced understanding of those you need to motivate.

The best football managers are known for their ability to recruit potential talent which then flourishes under their guidance. This ability is, to a large extent, dependent upon people skills. Identification of characters suitable for investment, in terms of development, is a more natural skill to those naturally interested in people.

The *Huddersfield Examiner* spoke of Herbert Chapman's 'ability to discover players who will earn laurels for themselves and their club; indeed his discrimination in the capture of budding players has been described as uncanny'. Bob Paisley's eye for a bargain was also legendary. During his spell, he recruited several players who

The top manager can also have a rebellious streak.

would go on to be considered players of the highest quality – Alan Hansen, Mark Lawrenson, Ian Rush and Graeme Souness among others.

As discussed above, the top manager can also have a rebellious streak. This comes from self-belief and a reluctance to follow the received wisdom. Such rebelliousness, allied to his people skills, allows him to recruit potential ignored by others. As Bob Paisley said: 'Some players can talk better than others, but we look for character in players. Scouts talk and tend to stick together in their opinions. If one of them condemns a player, they all tend to. If one says he's great, they'll all follow suit.'

Paisley's own description of his signing of Phil Neal from Northampton in 1974 indicates that he was alone among the top managers to spot the player's potential:

> **66**Apparently Phil had been set to join Aldershot (a lower league club). He might have got into habits he couldn't break and finished his career in the lower divisions, instead of coming here and playing 50 times for England. I saw him as a natural player who understood the game.**99**

We have mentioned how Brian Clough recognized John Robertson's potential talents and switched him from midfield to left-wing. Several players' careers were transformed this way under Clough. Tony Woodcock provides another example of Clough's ability to identify and concentrate on a player's strength – Clough converted him from a midfielder to a striker and he was selected many times to represent the England national team in this position. Woodcock himself wanted to play up front and had, in fact, been used in that position when on loan to Lincoln City, then under the guidance of debutante manager Graham Taylor. At Forest, Woodcock pressed his case with Brian Clough. 'What can you provide up front?' asked Clough. 'Goals,' replied Woodcock. As Woodcock himself tells the story, Clough turned away,

shrugged and told him to get on with it and prove it. Woodcock duly obliged.

Matt Busby converted John Carey and John Aston Snr from inside-forwards to full-backs. Paisley famously switched Ray Kennedy from striker to the left side of midfield: 'Moving Ray was the best switch I ever made. He had really lost his appetite for playing up front.' Kennedy went on to win numerous England caps in his new position. Football enthusiasts might be surprised to learn that the prolific goalscorer Malcolm MacDonald was a left-back until the Fulham manager Alec Stock spotted his potential as a forward in the late 1960s. Don Revie converted Terry Cooper from a moderate winger to an international left-back.

Perceptiveness is also the key to effective man management. Only the perceptive manager can see when someone needs a boost or which people will respond more to encouragement and which to chastisement. Ruud van Nistelrooy said of Alex Ferguson, 'Ferguson's strength is that he gets the best out of each player. He doesn't treat me the same as Roy Keane. He wants to know all about you and then build up a relationship'. John Murphy was a scout at Aberdeen under Ferguson. He said of him that he 'knows exactly how to handle players, knowing instinctively when to be firm with a player and when to ease up. It's a delicate balancing act.' According to Ray Clemence, Bill Shankly also possessed the ability to assess a player's mood:

66Shanks' greatest attribute was that he'd come in (to the dressing-room) and watch how everyone was getting ready and just speak to two or three of them. You could guarantee they'd be the ones who weren't quite there. He'd know, just by looking at them, that their mind wasn't on the game.99

He should know:

> **❝**I know because it happened to me on occasion. He'd sit next to you for five minutes and by the time he'd finished with you, you could think of nothing but getting on the pitch.**❞**

Different players need to be handled in different ways. Shankly said you 'must treat players like human beings. They have to be spoken to individually, some need to be spoken to strongly, others sympathetically.' Peter Taylor, Brian Clough's assistant for many years, said: 'Brian's man management would shape the player. He was brilliant at that. So many managers haven't got a clue how to handle players but Brian would bully one and cajole the others to get the best out of them.' Larry Lloyd, formerly of Nottingham Forest, provides us with one example of Clough's perceptiveness:

> **❝**John (Robertson) needed that 'well done', he needed that pat on the back. I couldn't give two monkeys whether he said 'well done' to me, and he knew that and he used to go the other way and give me a rollicking. Clough knew I used to fall for it, and running through that tunnel, my attitude was 'I'll show that big so and so.'**❞**

RUTHLESSNESS

Bob Paisley always came across as a gentle, quietly spoken but wise man. This was the public perception anyway. Graeme Souness painted a different picture:

&&He may be regarded by supporters and the public as a fatherly figure, but I can tell you one thing: he ruled Anfield with a rod of iron. If we looked as if we were becoming a little bit complacent or if we were not performing up to standard, Bob would say, 'If you have had enough of winning, come and see me. I will sell the lot of you and buy 11 new players.'99

One of Paisley's eventual successors at Liverpool, Gerard Houllier, claims that he has a ruthless streak beneath his affable exterior: 'I think I'm a very nice man but I can be a very nasty man if someone is not behaving right. If someone upsets the harmony of what we are trying to do, I am ten times nastier than anyone else.' Houllier cannot accept players whose primary responsibility is not to the team. When questioned about his acrimonious fall-out with David Ginola, Houllier is adamant that Ginola's part in the goal France conceded which eliminated them from the 1994 World Cup was not the bone of contention. Houllier explained the situation as follows:

&&Prior to the game, David spoke disrespectfully about certain of his team-mates who were selected ahead of him. As a consequence when the game was played, in Paris, in front of David's home crowd, they booed when Papin, for example, touched the ball. This did not help the team. David had put himself before the team – that is unacceptable.99

More recently Houllier again demonstrated his ruthless streak when he suddenly relegated his first-choice goalkeeper, Sander Westerveld, to third choice by buying two new goalkeepers on the same day. He was sold soon afterwards.

Ruthlessness alone does not make for good management. According to the great American football coach Bill Walsh, yet another balance a top manager must seek to strike is between sensitivity and ruthlessness (Rappaport, 1993):

> I have seen coaches who are simply too sentimental, who allow themselves to be too maudlin about 'breaking up the old family'. There is another kind who are severe, tough and hard-hitting. But they sacrifice the loyalty of the people around them. In that situation, people are always afraid that they are going to be the next to go. These coaches rarely have sustained success.

He offers this advice:

> Coaches must be decisive but be sensitive to the feelings, loyalties and emotions that people have towards one another.

The dips in the careers of Bill Shankly and Brian Clough were caused in part by an absence of this necessary ruthlessness. Liverpool did not win anything between 1966 and 1973. Shankly had delayed too long before breaking up the team which had brought him success in the mid-1960s. Peter Robinson, the Liverpool secretary at the time, says of Shankly: 'He did find it very difficult. He did tend to fall in love with his players and it was only results that eventually forced his hand.' Although he had earlier made provision for a rebuilding programme by investing in the club's youth system, it was only after an FA Cup defeat against Watford in 1970 that Shankly finally weeded out the old guard: 'If you can't make decisions as a manager, you're nothing, you should get out. We lost that game and I knew I had to start again.'

In his prime, Clough had no qualms about selling one long-standing player and introducing someone new in order to improve the overall standard of the team. Shortly after winning the championship at Derby in 1972, Clough signed David Nish to replace John Robson who had played in all but one of the championship-winning games. Robson was summarily sold to Aston Villa. After Nottingham Forest had won promotion to the First Division in 1977, Clough subsequently forced out several players to make way for new signings Kenny Burns, Peter Shilton and Archie Gemmill. Later in his career, however, Clough began to lose his ruthless edge. In Forest's relegation season in 1993, he kept faith with Mark Crossley, his goalkeeper, who had been suffering for a very long period from a severe crisis of confidence while continuing to play in the Forest first team. Martin O'Neill, a former player at Forest says:

> **66** Relegation would have been an impossibility under the man who managed me in the Seventies. You always felt he knew what was going on, even if you didn't particularly like him. His ego about criticism blunted his edge towards the end – how else could you explain keeping Crossley in the side? He was ruthless about such things in the great days. **99**

Jaap Stam was another player who fell foul of the ruthless touch of a manager when Alex Ferguson sold him to Lazio in Italy in August 2001. The move came as a total shock. Stam had been recognized as one of the best central defenders in the world

> *In his prime, Clough had no qualms about selling one long-standing player and introducing someone new.*

and one of the main pillars of United's success in recent years. Ferguson explained the dramatic decision by saying that he did not believe Stam to be playing at the standards he had previously set.

Jim Leighton was also the victim of Ferguson's ruthlessness. He had played for Aberdeen under Ferguson and the latter had later signed him to be the Manchester United goalkeeper. After an unconvincing performance in the drawn 1990 FA Cup Final against Crystal Palace, Leighton was dropped for the replay which took place a few days later. It is most unusual for established goal-keepers to be omitted from such a vital game and this incident is therefore recognized as a prime indicator that Ferguson was not afraid to deal ruthlessly with an individual if he believed that it was for the benefit of the team.

PRESENCE

We now come to the characteristic most commonly attributed to top managers and also the one most difficult to explain – presence or aura. To a certain extent a degree of ruthlessness and, indeed, a level of fear is intertwined with the presence of the manager. Great managers, by their presence, are able to demand the very highest standards and frighten/embarrass players who fall below those standards. An enduring image remains of Fabio Capello after Milan had won yet another Italian League title under his command in the 1990s. For a considerable time the players, all superstars of the football world, cavorted around the field cele-brating their success. Capello stood watching silently, nodding and chatting with fans and officials. After what Capello deemed to be a reasonable time, he whistled and gestured for the players to return to the dressing room. To a man these superstars responded immediately to the instruction. Capello turned and walked back to the dressing room totally confident that his players were behind him – and they were.

Almost every interview with a former player of Brian Clough seems to include an allusion to presence or aura. For example, Larry Lloyd said of Clough: 'When he walked into a room, you felt him there, even if you had your back to him. Clough had that aura and the players used to sit up and take notice of him immediately.' John O'Hare said: 'He could grab our attention in a couple of seconds. He had this presence.' Frank Clark said: 'When he walks through the door, the atmosphere is electric.'

The motivational impact of this characteristic is surely huge. These words from Clough's leading players encapsulate the secret of his amazing success as a manager. If players were in awe when all Clough had done was simply walk into a room, his effect on their level of effort and resulting performance on the field of play must have been immeasurable.

This presence is partly inexplicable – some people just seem to have it. However, it seems to be partly engendered by the perception of the players concerning the wisdom of the manager. This, in turn, seems to be reinforced by maintaining a distance from the players. We have seen how few seem to question Sven Goran Eriksson's tactics because of his perceived intelligent judgement. Bobby Charlton's stated belief that he always thought that Matt Busby knew best is also illuminating. Sean Fallon, Jock Stein's assistant at Celtic, said: 'All the players recognized his (Stein's) brilliant football mind. Any time he spoke, there was silence.'

To maintain this aura, managers often have been careful to maintain a distance from the players in social relations. David Miller (1971), Busby's biographer, said: 'He has always been slightly remote from the players with whom he has had this close mutual respect.' Alex Ferguson says of his players: 'I will never get close to them, I always keep my distance. Do I socialize with them? Never have, never will.' Distance contributes to the presence which top-class managers seem to possess. Where then does that leave first-time managers who are recruited from the ranks of the same organization to manage people of a similar age who were previously their colleagues and, possibly, friends?

This is certainly a tricky transition to make. Stan Cullis was appointed manager of Wolverhampton Wanderers in 1948 at the age of 31, having played with many of his new charges up until just a year beforehand. Right from the outset, Cullis asserted his new authority. He summoned all the players together. His speech, as recalled by Billy Wright, was as follows:

❝I want us to see eye to eye from the start. I want, and I am going to get, one hundred per cent effort from you all … If I get this support, you can take it from me that I will be one hundred per cent behind you. Nothing else is going to be enough.❞

They might all have been bosom pals before, but times had changed and Cullis immediately articulated the new reality in case anyone had failed to understand it. As his biographer Jim Holden puts it (2000):

❝The Cullis Creed was set in stone, and he never wavered from it during the next 16 years at Molineux. Total commitment to the cause brought total loyalty to a player from the Iron Manager. Lack of effort brought a swift and often miserable exit from the Wolves. The words which ring out from the speech are: 'And I am going to get.'❞

In other words, there was no question to be asked, no opposition to be brooked. Cullis went on to win three League Championships and the FA Cup twice in his time at Wolves.

LUCK

The final attribute of great managers is one that is rarely mentioned in business books because it is so intangible. Great managers need to be lucky. When asked which quality he most desired in his generals, Napoleon is reported to have answered – luck. If luck actually exists then the trick is to simply recognize those who have it and appoint them to decision-making positions in your organization. If, as we suspect, there is no such thing as luck, then why mention it? Because, in our view, what is actually happening is opportunism. A Chinese proverb describes luck as the place where preparation meets opportunity. Lucky people are those who prepare themselves to recognize random opportunities and then to seize them. As former prime minister John Major put it in *The Major Years* (BBC, 1999): 'If the ball comes your way, grab it.'

> Great managers need to be lucky.

It was not luck which won the European Cup for Manchester United in 1999 but their ability to apply pressure in the opposition penalty area and consequently amplify the odds in their favour. This does not, of course, *guarantee* success, but it alters the odds. England were not lucky to win their World Cup qualifying group in 2001 nor Germany unlucky to fail to do so. Over the eight games both had 'lucky' and 'unlucky' moments that balanced out. That final David Beckham goal in the match against Greece was the product of hours of training. Bryan Robson,

Manchester United's former Captain Courageous, tells how, even from his earliest apprentice days, Beckham would stay behind after training and practise his dead-ball kicking. As golfer Gary Player once famously said: 'The more I practise, the luckier I get.'

When Terry Venables handed the vital penalty kick to Gareth Southgate in Euro '96 it was not bad luck but bad preparation. Southgate had taken only one previous senior-level penalty and missed it. However, by comparison, Glenn Hoddle's decision to allow David Batty to take the crucial penalty in the World Cup '98 quarterfinal against Argentina made Venables seem well prepared. Batty had *never* taken a penalty at senior level. Neither agonizing exit had anything to do with luck, both were the result of inadequate preparation. Better preparation may not, ultimately, have resulted in victory, but it would have altered the odds. In simple business terminology, altering the odds can be translated into 'creating competitive advantage'. This is precisely why insider knowledge of trading intentions is banned – because it unfairly distorts the odds.

A simple example of the value of opportunism in the business arena is provided by the founder of Gemplus, one of the world's leading manufacturers of smartcards. The French company, founded in 1988 by Marc Lassus, a 40-something French physicist, now deals with industry giants Microsoft, Deutsche Telecom, Dell and Compaq. Was this the result of superb planning or luck? Neither, claims Lassus. 'I could sit back and tell you everything was completely planned. But I have to be honest – we haven't planned very much of this, and to some extent we still don't. We have just learned to be opportunistic.'

What this statement demonstrates is the need to prepare on two levels simultaneously, first the rational and second the random. Good managers will plan for the expected but will also plan to be

flexible and adaptable enough to seize the opportunities provided by the random. This is good management, not luck.

The perfect manager would, of course, have all the characteristics described above in the precise proportions designated by the perfect manager recipe book. Chairmen could then simply refer to the said recipe book and appoint the manager who would guarantee success. As we all know, in football and in business, nobody knows where the manager recipe book is hidden. Until we find it we must look at the characteristics and make judgements about potential managers in relation to the combination of characteristics we perceive as most significant. What *is* clear is that successful managers possess the full gamut of characteristics to some degree and they do, therefore, provide a useful checklist. The checklist is contained in the lesson on the next page.

Lesson

There is only one lesson from this chapter - look for these characteristics when selecting your next manager because those who succeed have them to some degree:

→ integrity
→ passion
→ ability to relax
→ analytical skills
→ hunger to learn
→ attention to detail
→ ability to get things done
→ insatiable appetite for accomplishment and results
→ self-belief
→ enthusiasm
→ people skills
→ ruthlessness
→ presence
→ luck

Managerial succession

PETER SALSBURY AND ROY EVANS HAVE A LOT IN COMMON. BOTH SPENT
their entire working lives in one organization and eventually
reached the top position. Their loyalty and commitment to the
cause were unquestioned. Both, however, were symbols of continuity, asked to preside over organizations in desperate need of
change. Both failed, victims of this mismatch. Their successors
were external hires, one Belgian, the other French. The symbols
of continuity had been supplanted by the foreign agents of
change.

Peter Salsbury was 51 when he was dismissed from his post as
chief executive of Marks and Spencer in September 2000. He had
worked for the company all his life, joining as a management
trainee from university in 1970, progressing from 'merchandiser
in ladies' outerwear' to 'executive responsible for developing
footwear' and then 'director of personnel' before controlling
'store operations, group estate, direct mail and franchise operations'. Salsbury's whole life revolved around the company. As one
journalist put it: 'Not only does Mr Salsbury wear M&S clothes,
eat M&S food and sit on an M&S sofa, but his wife and former
wife were both M&S women.' He was appointed to the top position in November 1998, taking over from Sir Richard Greenbury,
an M&S man for more than 40 years who had started his own
career in the company by sweeping floors at the age of 16.

Salsbury's elevation had been the result of a bitter boardroom row over succession, caused by the company's poor financial performance. Throughout 1998, the press had predicted problems looming for M&S. This was confirmed in November of that year when the company revealed its first fall in profits for seven years.

If M&S had heeded the lessons of football, Salsbury might not have been appointed in the first place.

Salsbury's appointment failed to arrest the slide. Two months after assuming control, he revealed the worst deterioration in M&S's trading history – profits were to be half those of the previous year. The poor results continued. Eventually, the company's non-executive directors decided that he was not the man for the job and Luc Vandevelde, a Belgian food retailer, was appointed as executive chairman. Vandevelde sacked Salsbury a few months later and took on the chief executive position himself.

If M&S had heeded the lessons of football, Salsbury might not have been appointed in the first place. Two weeks before M&S appointed Salsbury as chief executive, Roy Evans left Liverpool 'by mutual consent'. He was 50 and had been at Liverpool for 33 years.

Evans joined Liverpool as an apprentice player in 1965 when he was 17. He made 11 first-team appearances before Bill Shankly advised him at the age of 25 that he would be of more use to the club as a coach than as a player. He was reserve team trainer and then first team coach, with each role lasting for a spell of nine years. He became assistant manager for a year before eventually being appointed as manager in January 1994, replacing Graeme Souness.

Liverpool had been managed by insiders since Shankly had taken over in 1959. Shankly was replaced by Bob Paisley. Joe Fagan, who like Paisley had served Liverpool as part of the management team, took over for two years in 1983. He gave way first to Kenny Dalglish, who became player–manager, and then to Souness who, although appointed from outside the club, had made his name as a great Liverpool player during the 1970s and 1980s.

In the few years immediately prior to Evans's appointment, Liverpool had lost their pre-eminent position in English football. Between 1973 and 1990, they had won the league 11 times and had finished outside the top two positions only once. However, in the 1991/92 and 1992/93 seasons, they finished sixth. Winning the FA Cup in 1992 did not save Souness. He became the first Liverpool manager to be sacked since Don Welsh in 1956.

Despite the downward trend, the Liverpool board was not yet quite ready to appoint an outsider. But under Evans, Liverpool did not make the significant progress required. Although their league position improved (their final position was either third or fourth during Evans's four full seasons in charge), they finished an average of 11 points behind the winners, a considerable margin. Still the board hesitated, wary of breaking completely with the tradition which had served them so well in the past. Gerard Houllier, a French 'outsider', was eventually appointed as joint manager alongside Evans in July 1998.

This arrangement lasted just four months before continuing poor form prompted Evans's departure and Houllier's appointment as sole manager. The 40-year-old dynasty of succession was finally over. The point the board missed during its period of procrastination was that while internal succession had served them well *post-*Shankly, Shankly himself was originally an outsider. It was Shankly the outsider who had provided change when change was needed.

M&S was in the same position in November 1998 – a great organ-ization with a history of quality and achievement contemplating a downturn in fortunes. As at Liverpool, the M&S board was in denial over the reality of the predicament. They fudged the issue, preferring to paper over the cracks rather than confront the unthinkable, namely that the style and methods which had brought them so much success were now obsolete (and in Liver-pool's case, had actually been abandoned some years ago anyway, as we shall see later). Insiders weaned on the organization's ethos and its understanding of the past were not in an ideal position to realize this and so they appointed another insider who would inevitably be prone to the same fundamental weakness. The crit-ical eye of a complete outsider was required, and eventually sought.

The issue of internal versus external succession, which we will investigate in this chapter, is an obvious area where the experi-ence of football can guide the business world. What else can foot-ball teach us about the crucial subject of succession? For instance, what are the benefits of managerial stability? When is change advisable? Is a successful retiring manager the best man to select his successor? Should he stick around in some capacity after the new man takes the helm?

THE ARGUMENT FOR STABILITY

Eoin Hand, the former manager of the Republic of Ireland national team, once said: 'There are only two certainties in life: people die and football managers get the sack.' Between 1995 and 1998, 170 managers in the English Premier League and Football League were either dismissed or urged to step down. Consider-

ing there are only 92 clubs, this is some going. The only comparable wastage rate is in CEOs of top 100 companies.

However, the only periods of sustained one-club dominance in post-war English football, those enjoyed by Liverpool in the 1970s and 1980s and by Manchester United in the 1990s, were marked, contrary to the trend, by extreme stability of management tenure. Bill Shankly, who was largely responsible for building the foundations of Liverpool's success, was manager for 15 years until his voluntary retirement in 1974, when he was replaced by his long-time assistant and chosen successor, Bob Paisley, who served for nine years. Alex Ferguson has been manager of Manchester United since 1986.

It might be assumed that immediate and continued success led to this stability. However, both Shankly and Ferguson started inauspiciously. When Shankly was appointed in December 1959, Liverpool were in the Second Division and the club was in a hurry to return to a position more befitting its history and considerable support base. In his first full season at the helm, 1960/61, Liverpool missed out on promotion to the First Division by six points. Some directors, by all accounts, were having second thoughts about their appointment. Indeed, Walter Winterbottom, then manager of England, confirms that 'in those early days when things were not going too well, I urged the (Liverpool) chairman to stay loyal to Bill'. The following season, Liverpool finished eight points ahead of any rivals and were promoted. Two years later, in 1964, Liverpool were champions of England.

> Two years later,
> in 1964,
> Liverpool were
> champions of
> England.

When Alex Ferguson was appointed in November 1986, Manchester United had not won the League Championship in 19 years. Yet even throughout the club's lean years, it had the largest crowd attendances in England as fans flocked to see whether their team could recapture the glory years of the 1950s and 1960s under Matt Busby. By the time Ferguson took over, five managers since Busby's retirement in 1969 had already paid the price for failing to satisfy this huge expectation.

To the outside world, for some time it looked very much like Ferguson would be number six. In his first four seasons in charge, United finished eleventh, second, eleventh and thirteenth in the league table. In September 1989, United were beaten 5–1 by their local rivals, Manchester City. It seems difficult to imagine now, as United have been so dominant in recent years and the manager's wisdom is rarely questioned even by the press, but at that time many, probably most, supporters wanted Ferguson out. Indeed, at one United home match around that time, a large banner was unfurled at one end of the ground which said: 'Three years of excuses: Ta-ra Fergie.'

It is worth referring to a newspaper interview with him at that troubled time, just to remind ourselves how precarious his position actually was. A week after the Manchester City defeat, Ferguson was quoted as saying:

> **"** Believe me, what I have felt in the last week you wouldn't think should happen in football. Every time somebody looks at me I feel I have betrayed that man. After such a result, you feel as if you have to sneak round corners, feel as if you are some kind of criminal. **"**

The media pressure didn't help.

❝There's been a lot of speculation in certain papers over the last few days about my position at Old Trafford, some of it going as far as to link Howard Kendall with my job. At the very least it's unsettling and at worst it's been really mischievous. But I mean to be here, making a success of things, three years from now.❞

He added:

❝I know I have the courage to deal with all the sniping, but you worry about the effects on your family.❞

True to his intention, three years after the interview United had started the season in which they would eventually win the championship, heralding the start of the most successful period in the club's history. Interestingly, two huge clues to Ferguson's greatness are contained in that statement. First, his intense empathy with and feelings for the fans. In truth they were the only ones who completely shared his passion. Second was his strength of will – 'I mean to be here, making a success of things, three years from now.'

KEEPING THE FAITH

Why did the United board keep faith with Ferguson during those early years, despite media and supporter pressure to dismiss him? The first reason is that they craved stability after the turbulent post-Busby years and had learned from bitter experience that changing the manager does not necessarily bring success or even improved performance. Second, they had confidence in Ferguson because there was a strategic fit between his experience and their stated goals. Few other managers, if any, would be both similarly

suitable and available. Third, they were in the privileged position, denied to media and supporters, to witness at first hand the way that Ferguson was building the foundations for success. Lastly, lady luck intervened.

Were the United board right to be wary of change? The evidence suggests that they were. Ruud Kooning, a Dutch economist, wanted to see whether changing managers within companies affected performance. But he found it difficult to separate the managers' contribution from other factors, so he decided to concentrate on football instead. Analyzing the 18-team Dutch premier league between 1993/94 and 1998/99, when 28 managers were sacked, he concluded that there was no evidence to suggest that changing the manager induced an improvement in team performance. Kooning argued: 'Since it is not clear that results improve after a change of manager, it is likely that the board intervenes for other reasons. Fan and media pressure are strong determinants of the tenure of a football manager.'

Nevertheless, there can often be a very short-term improvement in form after a change of manager, probably caused by an increase in player motivation which in turn is prompted by reasons of self-interest. Established players are anxious to preserve their position and players who were out of favour with the previous management see a fresh opportunity to impress. For this reason, the decision to change the manager when there is a clear and very short-term goal, such as the team facing relegation with a few games to go, for example, does actually carry some logic. In fact, Crystal Palace's decision to sack their manager, Alan Smith, with only two games of the 2000/01 season left to play arguably saved the club from relegation.

However, Murray Steele, head of strategic management at Cranfield School of Management, believes that in the majority of cases

changing the manager serves little purpose other than to cause fresh upheaval and disruption: 'Change is all around and it is not always a good thing. Often it is not just a new manager that a club has to get used to but a whole new management team and a whole new philosophy of playing.' In other words, the advent of a new manager means that the club has to go back to square one and start again, in the process losing any underlying progress and momentum which might have been achieved by the previous manager. An article in the journal of the FA Coaches Association (*Insight*, Issue 4, Vol. 4, Autumn 2001) makes similar points and questions the value of changing managers.

Ferguson himself points out that even the threat of instability, let alone an actual sacking, can reduce the effectiveness of the manager's performance by undermining his authority:

  "Control gives the authority. And the one thing a player always respects is when he knows the manager is going to be his manager the next day. I think you see traces of that when a team's under pressure. They want to do well for the manager, but they know he is on a lifeline. They can see that his job is teetering. And thereby it dilutes the control of the whole place."

All this would be an acceptable price to pay if the manager was eventually sacked and replaced by someone much more suitable. Murray Steele goes on to say that 'the trouble for clubs which sack their managers is that there are not many good ones to choose from'. This is true, and while there may be some who have achieved at lower levels, there will be few who have the required experience to make them a realistic candidate to replace Ferguson as manager at Manchester United. As discussed in Chapter 2, Ferguson's specific experience at Aberdeen made him an ideal fit with

United's strategic goals. The United board, by sticking with Ferguson, demonstrated that current poor performance is insufficient grounds for dismissing the manager – there must be a willing alternative candidate who could represent a superior strategic fit.

Too often, football clubs give in to pressure to sack their manager because of a bad run of form. An unsuitable new appointment is then made hurriedly because the board does not want to give the impression to the outside world that it is not in control of the situation or is not acting decisively. Indeed, the reason why changing the manager does not usually work over the long term is not because change in itself is necessarily pointless. It is generally because the board does not fully contemplate the implications of sacking the existing manager and does not put enough time and thought into choosing the right successor. Consequently, the new man is appointed more in hope than expectation. Change for its own sake should never be an option.

> Too often, football clubs give in to pressure to sack their manager because of a bad run of form.

Another reason why the United board chose to offer Ferguson a three-year contract in the autumn of 1989 rather than sack him is because they had insider knowledge. As discussed in Chapter 5, soon after his appointment Ferguson launched into a thorough appraisal and then overhaul of the club's existing structures and, most importantly, its youth system. The supporters were not in a first-hand position to see this and therefore could not be blamed for not sharing the board's more optimistic view of the future.

This is where external communication becomes vital. When an organization enters into a long-term strategy which will not nec-

essarily bear short-term fruit, it must communicate the details of the strategy and any progress made, however small, to its support network – its shareholders for companies and also, for football clubs, its supporters. Failure to do so will create the pressure which could lead to a good manager being sacked and a sensible strategy being abandoned.

TURNING POINTS

The final reward for sticking with a manager comes, of course, when the prizes begin to arrive, be they championships or share dividends. Looking back over the period when things were not going so well, one can identify certain turning points. They are often referred to, in retrospect, as moments of luck. Ferguson's, for example, came in the form of a young 20-year-old. Striker Mark Robins left Manchester United in 1992 before United had won their first championship under Ferguson. After joining a succession of clubs, he now plays for Rotherham. Without his contribution, however, Ferguson would surely have been sacked over a decade ago and United's mission to win the League Championship might now be well over 30 years old.

United's poor run of form continued after the Manchester City defeat, and by the turn of the year the pressure on Ferguson was so intense that even United's board of directors would have found it difficult to be supportive for much longer. In January 1990, United were handed a difficult draw in the FA Cup, away at Nottingham Forest. The Cup was the last hope of any success for that season as United were out of contention in all other competitions. The media closed in for the kill, scenting certain blood.

Forest were the superior team for the majority of the game. However, Robins, by no means an established first-team player, scored the goal in the second half which won the game for United. That victory gave United renewed confidence and they went on to win the FA Cup that season. The following season, they won the European Cup Winners Cup and the self-perpetuating cycle of success had begun.

Howard Kendall, of Everton, was another whose moment of salvation is the stuff of football folklore. Everton, like United, had a tradition of success and achievement but had not won a major trophy since winning the League Championship in 1970. The club appointed Kendall, a former player in that championship-winning side, as manager in May 1981.

Throughout the 1970s, Everton had lived in the shadow of their local rivals, Liverpool, and the pressure on the board and any chosen manager to overturn that dominance was immense. But for the first two seasons under Kendall, it was the same old story, with Everton finishing eighth and seventh and Liverpool romping home to two titles. In January 1984, with the pressure on Kendall reaching fever pitch, Everton were drawn away to Third Division Oxford United in the League Cup. Defeat would have been a humiliation, but with a few minutes to go, and Everton trailing 1–0, Kendall's inevitable exit from Goodison Park seemed imminent.

At that point, the Oxford player Kevin Brock attempted a back-pass which was intercepted by Everton striker Adrian Heath. Heath scored, Everton won the replay, reached the final in that competition and won the FA Cup in the same season. The following season they won the first of two championships under Kendall and the European Cup Winners Cup. Is it luck or a steely nerve that makes the difference? Prob-

> The luck can't happen without the nerve.

ably a combination of both, but the luck can't happen without the nerve.

INTERNAL VERSUS EXTERNAL SUCCESSION

Should the successor come from inside or outside the organization? In a 1999 study (Lauterbach *et al.*), 165 top management successions in the US were analyzed. The purpose was to determine the relationship between the company's past performance and the source of the appointment and also whether external successions lead to different post-succession performances from internal successions. The study found that previously poor-performing firms appoint a significantly higher proportion of external successions and that, on average, external successions turn the firm around, while internal successions weaken the firm.

The first conclusion would seem logical. As the authors of the study point out: 'External successions are generally prescribed as a remedy for firm difficulties. When drastic changes are required, an external manager appears more promising because she or he is not [bound] by old policies and implicit contracts of the firm. An external succession can enrich the company with what it needs most – new perspectives, fresh ideas, and decisive actions.' However, when radical change is required, even suitable external candidates are difficult to find. As Nigel Nicholson, professor of organizational behaviour at London Business School, points out:

❝There is a global dearth of people who really have what it takes to be significant agents of change. The trouble is that corporate culture kills off these people before they can climb the ladder. It's usually the safe people who manage to get to the top.❞

The authors of the report (Lauterbach *et al.*, 1999) suggest that the second conclusion, that external successors perform better than internal successors, could be attributed to 'an agency problem'.

66 Sometimes, boards of directors let their personal acquaintances and relations with internal candidates distort their succession choice. Thus (1) some internal appointments are ex-ante poor choices, and (2) external successors (who overcome the bias against recruiting from outside) ought to be, on average, better managers and accomplish superior performances. 99

Can the experience of football contribute to this debate? Football clubs are smaller operations than many businesses and will therefore not offer a conveyor belt of potential internal successors anyway. It is generally only when a club has achieved its strategic aims in the recent past that the club considers an internal candidate, usually the former assistant to the retiring successful manager. It is in this specific area, then, namely the replacement of the retiring successful manager, that football can certainly teach us something.

Let us look at two such examples. First, the transition from Shankly to Paisley and subsequently other internal appointments at Liverpool. Why was the first transition so successful and where did it start to go wrong at Anfield? At what point should the club have, in retrospect, appointed someone who had no links with the club? Second, we shall examine an internal appointment which did not turn out well – Busby's replacement by Wilf McGuinness at Manchester United.

SHANKLY TO PAISLEY

Bill Shankly's retirement soon after Liverpool won the FA Cup in 1974 was a major shock to the football world. Would Liverpool be able to retain their position as one of the most successful English clubs of the modern period? The answer was a resounding yes. The initially reluctant Bob Paisley actually ended up with a superior managerial record to his predecessor. He presided over Liverpool's development from being one of a small number of top English sides in the late 1960s and early 1970s to being *the* dominant force in the domestic game and indeed in the whole of Europe.

The first point to emphasize about this particular internal promotion was that the successor, Paisley, possessed the attributes (see Chapter 3) which made him a natural manager, and the board recognized this. This was not an unthinking succession, and made only four years after the last high-profile internal promotion had failed at Manchester United, it was also a brave one.

Not only was Paisley a good manager in his own right, he actually learned from Shankly's mistakes so that in one vital area of management, recruitment, he became more than a match for his great predecessor. He made sure that players were replaced when they were past their best and that fresh blood was introduced regularly. Referring to Shankly's excessive loyalty to players in the late 1960s, Paisley said: 'It's essential to keep a turnover of players by bringing in new blood. Bill was living on what the team had done. I think it's got to be turned over year by year – an addition here, an addition there, sometimes several new faces at a time.' As highlighted in Chapter 3, Paisley's regular forays into the player transfer market were repeatedly inspired.

Another major factor in Paisley's success was that Shankly had bequeathed him a solid club structure with a heavy emphasis on the training and development of young players, many of whom were reaching full maturity as footballers at the time of the succession. Only three members of Paisley's team which won the European Cup in 1977 (Phil Neal, Joey Jones and Terry McDermott) had not been Liverpool players on Shankly's retirement in 1974. In other words, Paisley took over a club and a team on the rise.

A further aspect of Shankly's legacy was a great team spirit and a corporate ethos of hunger for success which would be strong enough to withstand a change in the identity of the manager. On Paisley's appointment, the players rallied around him, anxious that there should be no let-up in the quest for achievement. As Kevin Keegan says: 'I don't think anyone from outside would have had the courage to follow Bill Shankly, and we all said to ourselves: "Let's help the guy become a great manager."'

> On Paisley's appointment, the players rallied around him, anxious that there should be no let-up in the quest for achievement.

The final key reason why this particular succession came off so well was that Paisley's new authority was not undermined by the former manager's continued presence at the club. Shankly was a powerful personality whose presence dominated the club and the players had looked up to him for many years as their manager and mentor. Player Ian Callaghan's comments betray how difficult it would have been for Paisley to impose his authority if Shankly had been offered an opportunity to stay on at Anfield in another capacity: 'We all knew Bob so well – and some of us for a

long time – that it was difficult to suddenly adjust to calling him boss. We all called Shanks that!'

As it turned out, the Liverpool board decided against offering Shankly any position at the club, a policy with which Paisley agreed:

> **"** If he'd been elected to the Liverpool board, he'd have wanted to be in charge. And that's not a criticism. Being in charge was his strength and that's why Liverpool were so successful when he was manager … But at the same time I was in no doubt that I'd have to stand on my own two feet as Liverpool manager. **"**

Paisley was elected to the board of directors after his retirement as manager in 1983 and was asked to act as adviser to Kenny Dalglish when the 34-year-old, who had no managerial experience, was appointed as player-manager in 1985. But Paisley was a different character to Shankly. He was unobtrusive and willing to take a back seat unless his expertise was actively sought. As Paisley said: 'We were very different people. I'm delighted if no one recognizes me, whereas Bill wore steel caps on his shoes so people could hear him coming.'

Paisley's character was one reason why it was possible for him to stay on at Liverpool after his retirement as manager. Another is that when he retired, Liverpool's success was no longer principally associated with just one man. Whereas few could imagine Liverpool without Shankly in 1974, the club's continued success under Paisley had created the perception that it possessed a self-perpetuating formula for achievement, regardless of the identity of the manager. Consequently, Paisley would not in 1983 have had the same aura of a unique Midas figure which Shankly would

have had on his retirement. This aura would have made it virtually impossible for any new manager to assert his authority had Shankly stayed on at the club.

Under Joe Fagan and then Kenny Dalglish, Liverpool's success continued as they won the League Championship four times, the FA Cup twice and the European Cup before Dalglish resigned in February 1991. The commonly held assumption is that Liverpool's decline started during the reign of Graeme Souness, who appeared to make some poor recruitment choices in the player transfer market. However, it was Dalglish, despite his achievements as Liverpool manager and the excellence of the teams he managed at Anfield, who first disturbed the self-perpetuating formula which had served the club so well for a generation.

Throughout their period as the best side in England, Liverpool had been known for their ruthless efficiency, but not really for their flair or entertainment value. Professor John Williams, a football academic and co-author of *Passing Rhythms*, an examination of Liverpool's era of dominance, says: 'People forget how terribly dull they could be away from home. They weren't interested in scoring, just winning.' Joe Fagan described a typical Liverpool performance when he was manager as 'so efficient, it was chilling'.

Dalglish changed all that. Inspired by his signings John Barnes and Peter Beardsley, during the 1987/88 season Liverpool produced the kind of consistently breathtaking and thrilling football which English audiences had not witnessed since Alf Ramsey's success with a highly organized, efficient national team in 1966 had encouraged the subjugation of flair. One of Liverpool's performances in that season, a 5–0 victory against Nottingham Forest in April 1988, was hailed by many as one of the greatest performances ever by an English club side. Tom Finney, the former Preston and England playing legend, said the Liverpool performance that night was 'better than the Brazilians'. The Brazilians are synonymous in football with unpredictable invention, entertainment and winning. Liverpool teams may have been great under Shankly and Paisley, but they had never been compared favourably to the Brazilians before.

As we discuss in Chapter 5, Shankly, with the goal of European domination in mind, had developed a system of play which was designed for competition against foreign opposition. With English clubs banned from Europe after the Heysel disaster in 1985, Dalglish felt free to experiment with a new, more adventurous style of play, knowing that his players would be good enough to compete for domestic honours, whatever the system.

The appointments of Souness and then Evans after Dalglish's resignation were based on the illusion that continuity should be maintained. The truth was that this continuity had already been disrupted by Dalglish. The next managers were no longer asked to preside over a generation-old system and style of play. Internal promotions, which are designed to provide smooth transition and stability, had therefore ceased to be so relevant. It was not until it appointed Gerard Houllier in 1998 that the Liverpool board actually did what it should have done more than seven years previously – simply appoint the best manager available, whether he was a Liverpool man or not.

BUSBY TO MCGUINNESS

Unlike Paisley's succession of Shankly, Wilf McGuinness's tenure as Manchester United manager after Matt Busby's retirement in 1969 ended in failure only 18 months after his appointment. McGuinness had been a fine young player for United in the 1950s before injury terminated his career at the age of 22. United recognized his potential as a coach and he was given a position on the club's training staff. Busby nominated him as his successor and in April 1969 he was hurriedly awarded the position of chief coach in readiness to replace the retiring manager at the end of the season. In McGuinness's one full season in charge, 1969/70, United failed to make an impression, finishing eighth in the league. After an indifferent start to the next season, McGuinness was relieved of his duties and Busby was asked to return as manager on a temporary basis.

> The succession failed because all the factors which contributed to Paisley's success after Shankly's resignation were absent.

The succession failed because all the factors which contributed to Paisley's success after Shankly's resignation were absent. First, it is highly doubtful whether McGuinness himself had the necessary qualities to be a successful manager. Certainly, his managerial record after he left United was not wholly impressive. After achieving some success as a manager in Greece, he was appointed as manager of York City in February 1975 where he led the club to two successive relegations before his departure in October 1977. One could say in his defence that his experience at United had demolished his confidence, but we have seen in the previous chapter that one of the key attributes of a successful manager is the ability to bounce back after disappointment.

Second, unlike Shankly, Busby had not left a club and a team on the rise. United's capture of the European Cup in 1968 was not a launch-pad for further success but rather the swan song of a great team which had reached its peak two or three years previously. This view is confirmed by Bobby Charlton: 'It wasn't a strong side really (1968), not at all.' In Busby's final season, 1968/69, United finished a very disappointing eleventh in the league. Many of the previously great players such as Denis Law, Paddy Crerand, Nobby Stiles and Charlton were now past their peak and the genius of George Best had started to be tempered by the onset of alcoholism. What United actually needed after Busby's retirement was a fundamental rethink, not a seamless transition. Charlton continued: 'Things had dwindled over a period of years. I think McGuinness was chosen because the club had always had this family feeling, and the board were frightened that someone from outside would make too many sweeping changes. Who knows, maybe that's what was needed.'

This 'family feeling' which Charlton speaks of was also fast disappearing. George Best describes the atmosphere at the club at the time: 'Team spirit was falling apart. Cliques were forming, which we'd never had before, and there was a fair bit of back-stabbing going on.' Unlike at Liverpool in 1974, there was no strong bond among the players which could serve to ease the path for the new manager.

Busby had been manager at United for 24 years, had built three great teams, was idolized by the club's supporters and held in reverential esteem by the players, many of whom had played for him for a long time, and indeed, by the board of directors. There were not too many people around who could clearly recall a United without Busby, let alone a successful one. In short, Matt Busby *was* Manchester United in 1969. McGuinness's authority and the available scope to make his own impression as a manager were therefore seriously reduced by Busby's continued presence as general manager at the club.

Players with grievances approached Busby rather than the new manager. As McGuinness said: 'I was shafted by some of the players and by Matt Busby's willingness to listen to them all the time. They were going to him with this constant drip-drip of complaints. It was: "Wilf's not up to it, boss" or "The lads aren't happy," then "He's lost it with the lads," and "It's not going to work."'

This situation was exacerbated by the fact that Busby retained control of player contracts and recruitment and therefore it was he, not McGuinness, who had ultimate control over the players' careers. It was inevitable in retrospect that in the face of continued player dissatisfaction with McGuinness, or of supporter unrest, there would be a mass outcry for the board to turn again to Old Trafford's Midas figure, a scenario which ultimately materialized when McGuinness was relieved of his duties in December 1970. It is, of course, possible that the Liverpool board would have faced the same outcry to recall Shankly if Paisley had not taken to the manager's job as well as he did. However, unlike at Liverpool in 1974, Busby was close at hand to answer all those prayers for the great predecessor to return.

NAMING AN HEIR

Jack Welch is General Electric Co's midas figure. He increased the US company's market value by $500 billion and annual revenue by more than $100 billion from the time he took over as CEO in 1981. His opinion was held in such high esteem by the company that he was allowed to nominate his successor, which he duly did when he selected Jeffrey Immelt from a host of internal candidates in November 2000.

Was General Electric right to hand this privilege to Welch, a successful CEO entering into voluntary retirement? The experience

of football suggests that it might be, as long as the outgoing CEO was making his decision on the understanding that he would sever all formal links with the organization when the new man had been installed.

Busby nominated the insider McGuinness ostensibly because he wanted to continue what he understood to be a feeling of family at the club. As we have seen, here Busby was labouring under a misapprehension. In reality, he nominated McGuinness partly because an external successor would have been more likely to set his own agenda and Busby could not bear to relinquish completely his control over the running of the club which he had built up so painstakingly over such a long period. His personal agenda therefore ensured that he did not open up his mind to the possibility of the appointment of an external successor of proven quality, surely the right choice for United at the time.

> If the retiring successful manager is leaving completely, his judgement cannot be coloured by considerations of self-interest.

If the retiring successful manager is leaving completely, his judgement cannot be coloured by considerations of self-interest and therefore it surely pays at the very least to take note of his opinion. After all, he will know the club set-up and the players better than anyone. Shankly pushed his board in the direction of Paisley, a wise selection. Don Revie and Bill Nicholson both recommended Johnny Giles as their successor in the 1970s when they were leaving Leeds and Tottenham respectively. Their boards chose to ignore their recommendations. Leeds appointed Brian Clough instead, a disastrous appointment which lasted just 44 days. Their search for a worthy successor to Revie continued for many years subsequently. Tottenham surprisingly chose Terry Neill, who had managed Hull City during a number of mid-table seasons in the Second Division. Neill lasted two mediocre seasons at Spurs before accepting the post as manager of arch rival Arsenal. Giles himself went on to impress as manager at West Brom, winning them promotion in 1976 and consolidating their position in the top division the following year.

Manchester United were about to buck the trend by involving outgoing manager, Alex Ferguson, in the selection of his successor while offering him a continuing position in the club. The board was, at the very least, reluctant to keep Ferguson around when he would no longer be manager, but was forced down that route by fan and media power. But Peter Kenyon, Manchester United's CEO, vigorously defended the club's position to involve Ferguson in the selection process:

66 Sir Alex will obviously have input because he has done the job. We haven't decided whether he will be on the interview panel, but this is a unique opportunity. 99

He added:

66 When you replace one manager, it is normally because he has been replaced or left. We have got a manager who has great experience in doing the job, tremendous knowledge of the football club itself and someone who will continue to be involved in football. We are not going to throw that experience away but take heed of it. 99

With Ferguson signing a new three-year contract the process has gone on hold.

In this age of too few great managers for too many jobs, those few managers are increasingly able to control their own working lives. The elite band can decide when and if they want to move on, and the timing of that move. This might be good for the managers but it causes potential problems for the clubs because it can lead to lame-duck management. Massimo Cragnotti, president of the Italian club Lazio, for example, doubted the wisdom of keeping Ferguson around after he originally announced his intention to quit. He said:

❝Ferguson is an institution and it's difficult to send away such a man. But if they want to do the right thing for their club, United should change the manager quickly. The players lose their way when they know the coach is leaving. The team are like sailors on a ship who know the captain is about to jump.❞

Cragnotti was, of course, talking from bitter experience. His title-winning coach, Sven Goran Eriksson, announced his intention to leave Lazio to join England and the team's results nose-dived. They failed to progress in the Champions League, at huge cost to the club, and failed to successfully defend their title. Cragnotti believed: 'There was much to learn from [Lazio's] experience. United don't seem to have thought it out properly and they've done themselves damage as a result.' Interestingly, when Ferguson changed his mind about retiring he himself admitted:

❝In retrospect, I recognise it was a mistake to make the announcement of retirement plans so early. It changed the working atmosphere and may have derailed the players a bit.❞

As with most management issues what this chapter shows is that there is no magic formula to guide the succession process. What

is clear, however, is that it is not something to be taken lightly by boards of football clubs or corporate giants. Making the wrong choice can seriously damage the organization. While there is compelling evidence that changing managers does not necessarily provide immediate results, nobody would now dispute that Manchester United changing their manager to Alex Ferguson or Liverpool to Bill Shankly was a good decision. What must be recognized is that change for its own sake is rarely the answer.

Lesson

Provide stability but always be aware of the need for fundamental change. When that need becomes obvious, internal promotions may not be the answer.

PART III

Getting the job done

The life of a manager is very clear. If you win you are the best, if you don't you are out. That is normal.

Claudio Ranieri

Long-term strategy

WHAT SINGLE FACTOR MAKES PELE, ALI, REDGRAVE, NICKLAUS, TINA Turner and General Electric the greatest? Longevity! To be the greatest, it is not enough to be *simply the best* on any given day; that supremacy must be sustained over time. Of all the companies listed on the original FTSE 100, only GE survives. GE's managers come and go and are judged by how successful they are in continuing to ensure that GE survives and prospers. Arie de Geus, after a long career with Royal Dutch/Shell Group of Companies, achieved prominence as a management guru in collaboration with Peter Senge, the author of *The Fifth Discipline*, through their book *The Living Company* (1997). They argued in that book that the most effective way to think of companies is as organic entities which evolve by focusing on their longevity.

What de Geus found in his research was that the companies that survived over time were those that did not see themselves as primarily economic units to produce profits and value for the entrepreneur and the shareholder. The companies which survived saw themselves as living systems composed of other living systems – the people who worked for them and thus belonged to them.

The great football managers understand this. They too seek to build a viable system of long-term success. They differentiate themselves from the ordinary manager by their constant emphasis, through words and deeds, on the long term. This is apparent right from the early stages of their tenure. In business terms, although this year's profit and loss statement might be important and might buy you time to build real success, the more demanding and significant test of management is to set in place the fundamentals of the system, the structure and the style which will create sustainable prosperity. Since the success of a football team, like all other teams, relies very much on its human resources, the task of managers is to establish a structure and culture so powerful that long-term prospects cannot be jeopardized by the departure of any single individual.

> Long-term prospects cannot be jeopardized by the departure of any single individual.

Bill Walsh, the successful head coach of the American football team, the San Francisco 49ers, during the 1980s, when the team won three Super Bowl Championships in eight years, said this about the nature of winning:

66 Winning does not necessarily mean being the victor in every single game. It is not winning every game at any cost. We have to remind ourselves that it is not just a single game we are trying to win. It is a season and a series of seasons in which the team wins more games than it loses and each team member plays up to his potential. 99

He added:

66 If you are continually developing your skills and refining your approach, then winning will be the final result. 99

Focusing on the long term is not easy for a manager when besieged by short-term pressures. In business, shareholders demand short-term capital gain and an annual dividend. In football, impatient supporters are not easily placated by talk of the long term when their team has just been beaten heavily by their hated local rivals. The criticism of shareholders or supporters (something of a hybrid between shareholders and clients) can easily lead to the removal of a manager or a chief executive.

When managers constantly feel under pressure of losing their jobs, the idea of long-term planning can seem academic and impractical. Graham Barrow has been the manager of non-league Chester City and league clubs Wigan Athletic and Rochdale. His comments, when manager at Wigan, convey well how the imperatives of the short term can dominate any long-term vision:

❝Long-term planning isn't always feasible. I have to listen to the youth development officer saying he's got the best 14-year-old, but sometimes I think, 'What use is that to me at the moment?' It's hard to believe I will still be here to see him make his debut. You can become too involved with youth development, because young players don't win you anything.❞

Insecurity breeds short-termism. In this environment, the manager may as well concentrate only on short-term success. If it is true that the only certainty in football is the sack and the manager believes he will be dismissed at some stage anyway, he needs to ensure that he has achieved some short-term success which he can point to on his CV. The long term thus takes a back seat, as David Pleat, a manager at many top-level clubs over the years and still on the staff at Tottenham Hotspur, points out: 'Some managers are driven by fear. They go for the expedient way of playing football, get success as quickly as possible, and then move on.' While Pleat implies a negative bias to the comment, it remains a sensible and logical strategy for self-preservation, but not greatness.

There are, therefore, two necessary conditions which enable thoughtful and patient long-term planning. The first is the confidence of the support network – the employer, the shareholders and the supporters. Gaining the confidence of this complex constituency of employer, shareholder or supporter requires frequent and effective communication by the manager. Everybody needs to be informed of the goals of the management and the timescale and the methods for the achievement of these goals. If this communication is absent and the support base not established for the long haul, then lack of early success will lead to irresistible, insupportable external pressure and the cycle of short-termism will continue. These issues are discussed more fully in Chapter 4.

> Everybody needs to be informed of the goals of the management and the timescale and the methods for the achievement of these goals.

The second necessary condition is that the manager has the intellect, self-confidence and commitment to think and act long term. Needless to say, if enough time, effort and thought are spent finding the right manager at the outset, this will create a whole atmosphere of confidence, which will in turn create the breathing space essential to the painstaking building of long-term success. How many times have organizations rushed into the appointment of a manager or key executive, only to be back at square one a short time after, this time facing additional pressure for short-term success from shareholders or supporters?

PARAMETERS OF SUCCESS

If, then, the organization recognizes the need for a manager with the intellect and commitment to act long term, what should be the first imperative for building that long-term structure? It is the establishment of the parameters of success and their communication to the necessary audience. What precisely is the definition of success for that club and when can it be achieved?

Herbert Chapman is one of only three managers in history who have managed to win the League Championship with two separate clubs. His success in the inter-war years revolutionized the perception of the manager within football by making apparent the positive effect an active manager can have. Having won the championship twice with Huddersfield Town, he became manager of Arsenal in 1925. Arsenal had been struggling and had narrowly missed relegation from the First Division in 1924. His language from the outset of his tenure betrayed a watchful consideration of the long term. He told the supporters in the club programme on his appointment: 'Do not expect too much in too little time. It will be five years before a major honour is won.' Arsenal duly won the FA Cup in 1930.

Gerard Houllier took over as sole Liverpool manager in November 1998. Interviewed at the end of the 1999/2000 season, still not having won a trophy, Houllier fended off criticism of the lack of short-term success and was at pains to stress the positive progress made towards the achievement of a stated, explicit, long-term goal:

❝I have to look at the overall picture and what I am engaged in at this club is a four-year strategy to re-establish Liverpool among the foremost clubs in the country. But my job is to view the season from an

overall perspective and we have made sound progress. We have already got 13 points more than we did last season and we have a higher league position.**"**

Liverpool went on to make substantial further progress in the 2000/01 season, winning the Worthington Cup, the FA Cup and the UEFA Cup. What both Chapman and Houllier established were challenging yet realistic goals. When setting a long-term strategy, it is necessary to acknowledge at the outset the limitations of the organization and to know what it can and cannot feasibly achieve. Failure to do so will result in imprudent decision making.

MANAGING EXPECTATIONS

In football, managing expectations is even more important than in business. Supporters hold shares in paradise, a hard expectation to realize. At those clubs which have enjoyed success in the past, supporters may wonder why it is so difficult to recapture glory days, irrespective as to how unrealistic such expectation might be.

> Supporters hold shares in paradise, a hard expectation to realize.

Dario Gradi, of Crewe Alexandra, is the longest-serving manager at any club in the English league. He took over the role in 1983. Gradi is convinced that the management of expectations is the key to long-term viability and consequently relative success. He believes that the board's modest ambitions, entirely commensurate with the history and size of the club, have helped him to build gradually the foundations of long-term success:

❝Unrealistic expectations are pointless. When I first came to Crewe in 1983, I asked the directors what they expected of me as manager. They said that if we finished fifth from bottom – in the old Fourth Division – they would give me a contract for next season. If we finished in the bottom four they would probably give me a contract anyway.**❞**

He is clear about his goals:

❝The aim was to keep them out of financial trouble, and that is still a major consideration. If we have some success along the way, that's terrific – and we have managed to do so.**❞**

Crewe have climbed two divisions under Gradi and have stabilized as a solid First Division team. Graham Taylor similarly defined what he considered success to be at Watford. He argued that, for Watford, to be a constant top 30 club must be a sign of success. That may mean yo-yoing between the Premier and the Nationwide, but for Watford that must be seen as success. The occasional sojourn in the Premiership injects sufficient cash to enable the realization of Taylor's ambitions. Whether his vision is shared by chairman Elton John and new manager Gianluca Vialli remains to be seen.

A classic example of how misplaced ambition can lead to hasty and wrong decisions is the experience of Manchester City in the 1990s. In November 1990, the 34-year-old Peter Reid was appointed to his first position as manager. Under Reid's guidance in three seasons at the helm, City finished fifth, fifth and ninth in the Premier League. Given City's miserable performance during the 1980s when they spent a few seasons outside the Premier League, a realistic board of directors might have been expected to

be more than satisfied. The memory of the great City team of the late 1960s, however, still imbued the club with a sense that they should be competing for the very top honours. The capture of the League Championship in 1993 by City's arch rivals, Manchester United, was too much to bear and Reid was sacked in August. As Chris Muir, one of City's directors at the time, said:

❝It was a disaster for us. Peter Reid had staked so much on outdoing United and now they had beaten us to the championship. He was crestfallen and I think we knew it was extremely significant for the club.❞

The City team deteriorated in the coming seasons, even suffering the ignominy of being relegated two divisions. Reid took over at Sunderland where a more realistic and supportive board has helped him to consolidate the club's position in the top half of the Premier League. City have again returned to the Nationwide League.

Managing expectations is also crucial to avert damaging pressure and to give time for the longer-term changes to develop. Gerard Houllier is a master of the art. There was little media or fan talk about him being sacked before he achieved success because he was managing expectations. Even after his team had won several trophies in 2001, he referenced Ferguson, who by that stage had become the benchmark for long-term success, in order to dampen the expectations of the fans which was reaching fever pitch. Houllier explained:

❝Alex (Ferguson) took seven years to win the championship and I have been here two-and-a-half. Give me a bit of time. If we manage to keep our players and get one or two more signings, then in two or three

years we can be very strong, but you can't programme success, you can only prepare. I am preparing.▶▶

David O'Leary has also diverted attention from the progress of his team by playing down their aspirations. He has constantly spoken about how young his side is, how inexperienced, how his squad cannot compete with the big-spenders. This picture conveniently ignores the fact that he spent close to £90 million on new players in the three years to November 2001.

Expectations need managing at the other end of the league table. If expectations are set too low, that in itself can become a self-fulfilling prophecy. When you set your aims, it is better to aim higher than the minimum in order to give yourself room to manoeuvre. Sam Allardyce, Bolton's manager, said prior to his team's entry into the Premier League: 'We shouldn't be saying to ourselves that our aim is to finish fourth from bottom.' David Sheepshanks, chairman of Ipswich Town, explained his philosophy when his team were promoted to the Premier League:

◀◀Arriving in the Premiership we needed a new plan and I am a great believer in aiming high. It's better to aim high and miss than aim low and achieve it. We budgeted to finish seventeenth, but we aimed to finish eleventh this season. The longer-term aim was to qualify for Europe in 2003. There is not enough long-term planning in football. Clubs want success today, and if not today, tomorrow. Here we have an ethos of continuous improvement.▶▶

Ipswich qualified for Europe two years ahead of schedule, in 2001.

BEST PRACTICE

Crucial lessons can be learned from other successful organizations in devising long-term strategy. The wheel does not have to be reinvented. Gerard Houllier's efforts to bring success back to Liverpool have relied much on the methods used by Alex Ferguson in building the great Manchester United team of the 1990s. For instance, as we discuss later, Ferguson has stressed the importance of bringing young players through the system from an early age. These players feel an affection and loyalty for the club and serve to create a positive corporate ethos. The homegrown players are then joined by carefully selected top-level recruits from the domestic league or abroad, creating a potent mix of talent and team spirit and understanding.

It is a lesson which Gerard Houllier has heeded, with the likes of Steven Gerrard, Jamie Carragher and Michael Owen prominent in his first-team squad alongside players recruited from outside. He states: 'What I am looking for is a balance within the squad, and I think we have that mix of good overseas players and some we have produced ourselves. I think it is important that you develop your own players.' Of course, Houllier did not appreciate the value of youth development only from Ferguson. As the manager of the French Under-18 squad (where Thierry Henry was his captain) as well as the director at their school of excellence, Houllier already understood the bond that is created when players are brought up together.

> Houllier already understood the bond that is created when players are brought up together.

Another crucial concept which Houllier shares with Ferguson is the idea of the large squad, and especially the four-striker rotation system. Ferguson, realizing the need to keep his strikers fresh and competitive and mindful of possible injuries and suspensions for important games, introduced the striker rotation system fully in 1998 when he signed Dwight Yorke to add to Andy Cole, Ole Gunnar Solksjaer and Teddy Sheringham, all top-level strikers. From these, Ferguson would pick two for any one game and rest the other two. The system was a major factor in United winning the treble in the 1998/99 season. Houllier, seeing that he had only two top-level strikers in Robbie Fowler and Michael Owen, added Emile Heskey and Jari Litmanen to his squad: 'I have a good memory of games when we didn't have enough strikers because of injuries, so it is vital for us to have at least four here. This is something we have always stressed.' Owen emerged from a slump just as Litmanen was sidelined for the rest of 2000/01 season. This rejuvenation culminated in the two-goal Cup-winning performance in May 2001. When Fowler was eventually sold in late 2001, he was almost immediately replaced by the recruitment of Nicolas Anelka.

The last team before Manchester United to achieve success over a prolonged period was Liverpool in the 1970s and 1980s. A brief interruption to their run of success occurred in the late 1970s when Nottingham Forest, managed by Brian Clough, won the English League once and then the European Cup twice. As Frank Clark, a Forest player of the era, points out, Forest's achievements owed much to studying and deriving best practice from their rivals at Liverpool:

❝The year we won the title (1978), we got people forward and ran teams off the pitch. Then we developed an almost European style very close to the way Liverpool play ... We would tend to sit back with nine men behind the ball and invite teams to come at us. For many years,

Liverpool had been the masters of soaking up punishment. We developed that and out-Liverpooled Liverpool. **99**

LAYING THE FOUNDATIONS

After setting the goals and the timescale for the long-term strategy, top managers have sought to put in place the foundations upon which success can be painstakingly built. Seeing the big picture and setting the goals is the easy part. Establishing and consolidating the necessary foundations requires dedication, professionalism and an almost obsessive eye for detail.

The single, most important, component of the foundation is the appointment of the staff to support the manager. A support team must be assembled which the manager knows and trusts, the members of which share his vision and complement his attributes. Only in this way is it possible to produce a complete managerial unit. Intuitively and rationally, all top managers understand this. The important issue of delegation and managerial support will be discussed in greater detail in Chapter 6.

PERSONAL DEVELOPMENT

Another component of the foundation is the investment in training facilities where players, football's human resource, can hone and improve their skills for years to come. The *Huddersfield Examiner* reported in 1925 that the players in Herbert Chapman's Huddersfield team 'had expert and scientific training methods to preserve and lengthen their careers'. Soon after his arrival at Liverpool in 1959, Bill Shankly complained that the training ground at Melwood was 'a wilderness … it was in a terrible state'. At Shankly's request, the board made the necessary investment to

upgrade the facilities: 'Shanks transformed Melwood,' recalls Roger Hunt, a Liverpool player of the time. 'He introduced new training boards that we used in various exercises, he got an all-weather pitch, brought it up to scratch.'

The great managers of the modern era have also understood the potential long-term rewards of investing in the development of players' skills. Sir Alex Ferguson has helped to conceive and design Carrington, a state-of-the-art training complex, complete with acres of football pitches and top-notch indoor and medical facilities. After taking over at Arsenal in 1996, Arsene Wenger soon realized that the training facilities at London Colney were inadequate. Together with the Arsenal chairman, Peter Hill-Wood, he studied the best aspects of training facilities at top European clubs renowned for their player development, such as Auxerre, Nantes and Bayern Munich. After 18 months of meticulous planning, the new site boasting the very latest in modern technology and sports science was opened in October 1999. As Wenger points out, the new complex serves not only to improve current players' skills, it will also 'be a big attraction for players who may come to Arsenal from outside the club. They will be very impressed by the facilities that are available for them and perhaps more likely to sign for the club.'

It is possible to be too concerned with just 'doing the job' on a daily basis.

However, the most modern facilities and training methods will be wasted if the culture of an organization is not directed towards increased professionalism and a collective focus on progress. It is possible to be too concerned with just 'doing the job' on a daily basis, dealing with problems and issues ad hoc, with no real thought for the opportunities which might exist for the organization to improve its overall

working methods. Addressing the organization's whole attitude to issues of training and personal development is a key fundamental in long-term strategy in a people business. As Ferguson says:

❝I think the main difference between here and the Continent is the preparation the Europeans put into the game. We have to get away from the mentality as kids of 'just playing the game'. Just because you are playing football doesn't mean you are a bloody footballer. That comes from sheer practice.**❞**

He adds:

❝If you say, here is a ball, go and do what you want to do, a lot of players in Britain just end up shooting the ball in the net. Yet there is this big piece of football ground where you can learn to master the skills, the balance, the movement. You have to lay down the fundamentals of practice.**❞**

Such is the determination of great managers to lay the right foundations for long-term success that no detail, however seemingly insignificant, is overlooked. For instance, it is no coincidence that two of the truly great modern managers, Bill Shankly and Don Revie, even changed the colour of the strip their team traditionally wore, in order to gain a potential psychological advantage. Shortly after taking over the helm at Leeds United in the early 1960s, Don Revie ordered the club's home strip to be changed from blue to all-white, thus mimicking Real Madrid, who at the time were the dominating force in European football. Ron Yeats, who played under Shankly at Liverpool, recalls the time when

Liverpool changed their strip from red shirts and white shorts to the now famous all-red:

❝I can remember the day that Shanks came to me after training and said he wanted me to try on a shirt. Then he said, 'Yes, aye. That's what we'll play in from now on. It'll make the whole team look huge.'❞

YOUTH DEVELOPMENT

Central to any long-term strategy in an industry which is very reliant on its human resource is the development of an excellent youth system. Any organization in such an industry can be deeply vulnerable to the defection of key individuals. It is therefore the task of the management to institutionalize the organization's method of operating, so that success can be sustained even in the face of constant turnover of personnel. By far the most effective way of achieving this is by placing great emphasis on educating talented young recruits in the ways of the organization from the very moment they arrive. Not only does it protect the organization against defection, it is also highly cost effective. Gerard Houllier explains the cost effectiveness as follows:

❝We at Liverpool have spent £12 million on an academy, but it's worth it. If you take five 11-year-olds, you'll make two or three pros. Two won't make it, maybe injured, maybe mental weakness. But the two or three who do make it will pay off the investment.❞

Matt Busby is the manager most famed for prioritizing a youth programme as the primary factor in the development of long-term strategy. Taking over at Manchester United in 1945, he arguably built three great teams – the FA Cup winners of 1948, the 1950s team which twice won the League Championship and was virtually destroyed in the Munich air crash of 1958, and the team which won the European Cup in 1968. In each of these teams, not more than four players, and usually fewer, had been recruited from another club, the rest having been raised through the United system. 'If my club decides to buy a player,' Busby once said, 'it is because every other method of filling a place in the Manchester United team has failed.'

> It still seems remarkable that Busby managed to win Europe's premier club competition merely ten years after the majority of his 'Busby Babes' died tragically at Munich.

It still seems remarkable that Busby managed to win Europe's premier club competition merely ten years after the majority of his 'Busby Babes' died tragically at Munich. However, he had created an environment in which success could be regenerated eventually. As his biographer, David Miller, describes it:

66 Busby formed a team which created a conveyor belt carrying the most talented boys in England, Scotland, Ireland and Wales from the classroom to the Manchester United first team. It was a system, a machine, which other clubs came to fear and resent. 99

Busby himself said:

66 I did not set out to build a team: the task ahead was much bigger than that. What I really embarked on was the building of a system

which would produce not one team but four or five, each occupying a rung on the ladder, the summit of which was the first XI.**"**

Another issue which is often lost in the youth development debate is the attachment of the community (the fans) to the players perceived as 'home-grown'. True fans know of players in the youth teams and reserves; they watch them grow up; they try to spot the stars of the future and identify with them when they reach the first team. Even if such players are not natives of the area, they are adopted as such. Of course, if such a player is genuinely a home-town boy – a Gerrard or a Scholes – so much the better!

> Not only does a youth system produce relatively cheap capital assets (the players), it also feeds and sustains the stakeholder base (the supporters).

The fact that all the players in Celtic's 1967 European Cup-winning team were born within 30 miles of Parkhead is often commented upon. Bobby Lennox, who was born the furthest away (30 miles), was known as 'the foreigner' to his team-mates.

It appears, therefore, that not only does a youth system produce relatively cheap capital assets (the players), it also feeds and sustains the stakeholder base (the supporters). Finally, it tightens the bond between club and community so necessary to the long-term viability of the club. One way in which clubs such as Real Madrid and Juventus can maintain huge and continual overdrafts is with the forbearance of the financial community. That is possible because *not* to support the club would be considered scandalous.

BENCHMARKING

As discussed earlier, the two teams in the post-war era which have managed to achieve the longest period of sustained dominance over their rivals were Liverpool in the 1970s and 1980s and Manchester United in the 1990s. During the years 1973 to 1990, Liverpool won the League Championship 11 times, the European Cup four times and the FA Cup once. During the years 1990 to 2001, Manchester United won the League Championship seven times, the European Cup once and the FA Cup four times. These two teams provide the benchmarks for continued success. How can we explain this phenomenon, achieved despite a constant turnover of playing personnel?

Many people might argue that it was money which bought success at both clubs. Indeed, it is true that Liverpool and Manchester United especially have massive numbers of followers and, therefore, considerable financial resources. It is also true that a club cannot hope to achieve top-level success without being able to compete in the player transfer market and to pay the huge salaries which the best players demand. However, many clubs have spent large sums of money on players and not achieved this kind of success. Indeed, Manchester United, the wealthiest club in the country, were unable to win the League Championship for 26 years from 1967 to 1993, despite regular forays into the player transfer market.

In fact, if one looks at the money clubs spent on players in the three years prior to 2001, six clubs spent considerably more than Manchester United, yet United won the League Championship in 1999, 2000 and 2001. Leeds United, Liverpool, Chelsea, Arsenal, Newcastle United and Aston Villa spent almost £400 million in total in this period in their pursuit of success, compared with United's £45 million.

Newcastle United, under the management of Kevin Keegan, spent approximately £40 million between the start of the 1993/94 season and the summer of 1996, more than any other club during this period, in their pursuit of the League Championship. Keegan famously abandoned the reserve team and youth structure at Newcastle, preferring to concentrate solely on his expensively recruited first-team squad. This policy made short-term success an absolute necessity in order to fund the continuation of this strategy. As it happened, the team failed, Keegan resigned and the club was left with debts, no talented youngsters and a group of disgruntled and highly paid stars. Having finished second in 1996 and 1997, Newcastle slumped to 13th in the league table in 1998.

We would therefore argue that the most significant determinant of the prolonged success of Liverpool and Manchester United in their respective periods is indeed the accent on the recruitment and education of young players. It is worth examining the early years of both eras in more detail to see the positive repercussions of each club's youth strategy.

LIVERPOOL – THE EARLY YEARS

Although Liverpool actually won more trophies after 1974, when Bob Paisley took over as manager, it was Bill Shankly who laid the foundations for success from 1959 to 1974. Shankly really started to concentrate on Liverpool's youth system in the mid-1960s. His mostly bought team had won the League Championship in 1964 and 1966 and the FA Cup in 1965. By the late 1960s, the team was in decline and Shankly realized that he did not have the ready-made replacements. Dominance could not be readily sustained without the periodic introduction of fresh youngsters who had learned how to play the way he wanted. Although players could be bought in the transfer market, it would take time for the

signings to learn the Liverpool style, and as Shankly noted, he 'couldn't buy £100,000 players and play them in the reserves'. He had learned his lesson and began to lavish attention on the club's youth policy.

Geoff Twentyman, appointed chief scout in 1967, acknowledged Shankly's preference for 'getting them young so he could mould them into what he wanted'. Shankly exhorted the staff responsible for the youngsters' education in the reserve and youth teams to educate them in his football philosophy:

66 The first result I wanted to know after the match was from the reserves. Get the boys into the habit of winning, it's a good habit. It doesn't matter how you win at first, but as you start getting results, you gain confidence and can change your pattern. You entertain as well as win. I didn't want them in the first team until they could do both. 99

He made it clear what he wanted:

66 I want a side to bring character and excitement to their performances, this is what gives me enthusiasm and energy. 99

The young players introduced to the club in the late 1960s and early 1970s, such as Alec Lindsay, Steve Heighway, Phil Boersma, Brian Hall, Ray Clemence and Kevin Keegan, became the cornerstone of the successful Liverpool team for many years after. These players had either been developed through the youth system or bought relatively cheaply at a young age from smaller, more provincial clubs and then gradually groomed for the Liverpool first team.

MANCHESTER UNITED – THE EARLY YEARS

Alex Ferguson soon began a reorganization of the youth system at Manchester United after his appointment as manager in 1986. He had gradually built success at his previous club, Aberdeen, by implementing an efficient youth policy. His Aberdeen team which had won the European Cup Winners Cup in 1983, a phenomenal success for such a provincial club, contained only three bought players. He was determined to replicate this success at United.

When he took over, he realized that the squad he had inherited from the previous manager, Ron Atkinson, was not young enough to achieve sustained success:

❝I looked at them and asked, how can they win the league? Too many of them were around the 30-year mark. I knew that if we didn't win the championship in the first two years with them, then we'd be in trouble.❞

He soon laid down the law:

❝I called all the scouts together and told them that I didn't want the best kid in the street, but the best in their town or city. We were not interested in them having a nice easy job looking at kids in the local park. I told them to get off their backsides and go and find me the best.❞

A large staff – Brian Kidd, Nobby Stiles, Eric Harrison and Jimmy Curran – was given the task of laying the foundations for United's future. Ferguson's long-term vision was handsomely rewarded. By Christmas 1990, the club was beginning to reap the dividends. Ferguson told the *United Review*:

> ❝Next season we have the best group of schoolboy players coming to Old Trafford we have ever seen. I am particularly thrilled by the quality of the boys who will soon be here, and I see it as a result of our reorganization.❞

Looking back on this time, Ferguson says:

> ❝We had a crop of young players developing who were outstanding and we knew that we would have a secure future with them. It was the fruit of hard work, total dedication, long hours and self-belief.❞

Out of the United team which won the FA Youth Cup in 1992, five players – Ryan Giggs, David Beckham, Gary Neville, Paul Scholes and Nicky Butt – have had crucial roles in United's period of dominance.

The long-term approach held by Shankly and Ferguson was exemplified by the very gradual introduction of young players into the team. Both managers were anxious not to burn out the young players at an early stage of their careers by playing them too much. They were to be fixtures of the team for many years and therefore had to be protected. They were given time to acclimatize to the huge physical and mental demands of first-team football.

Brian Hall, the former Liverpool player, says that he got 'a few games as substitute in 1968/69, had a poor season the next year and had a few more appearances as substitute, but it was 1970/71 when we all started to come through'. In 1994/95, for United, David Beckham played only two games, Paul Scholes six games and Butt 11 games. In the following season, all three played in the great majority of games as United won the League Championship and the FA Cup.

Both Shankly and Ferguson used the youth system to build their long-term vision of success in European competition. They craved a different style of play, a more patient, passing game with an emphasis on possession of the ball, which they believed would be more effective in Europe. This type of football was not widespread in England and hence could not be easily achieved solely by signing players from other clubs who had already been brought up in the British style of play. However, if a batch of youngsters emerged playing the way they had been taught, this would serve to establish an entire self-perpetuating culture at the club for many years – the next crop of young players would learn from them and so on.

> Both Shankly and Ferguson used the youth system to build their long-term vision of success in European competition.

Geoff Twentyman said: 'Collective play, whereby we play from the back, came in more with the new team. We learned in Europe that you can't score a goal every time you get the ball … It's cat and mouse, waiting for an opening. It's been built up over the years.' Emlyn Hughes, the former Liverpool player, believes that 'the team learned how to play in Europe from the 1960s side, learning from defeat. Playing in Europe was completely different. We went and slowed it down – the continentals were better passers so we had to match that … It was Shanks' idea, he made us into a great side.'

United were beaten heavily by Barcelona in 1994. Stephen Kelly (1997) later wrote: 'Ferguson heeded the lessons, ordering his youth team coaches to begin training the youngsters in possession football in their own half, and then learning how to release the long, quick, accurate pass that fires up an attack.' Five years later, Ferguson's team won the European Cup.

147

In summary, the effort invested in the Liverpool and United youth systems had two principal ramifications. First, it enabled the club management to inculcate a method of operating which would enable the organization to tackle its long-term goals with some hope of success. Second, it reduced the organization's dependence on one or a group of key individuals. If a successful system has been established in which talented young players are constantly coming through the ranks, trained in the club's style of play, then supposed star individuals become more dispensable. Of the United squad which won the League Championship by a wide margin in 2001, only two, Ryan Giggs and Denis Irwin, played a part in United's first League Championship of their current successful sequence in 1993.

Another lesson which can be derived from successful youth policies is the tireless dedication which went into them. Ferguson's comment to his scouts that he did not want them to 'have a nice easy job looking at kids in the local park' and that they should 'get off their backsides and go and find me the best' is typical of this commitment. The club, Ferguson believed, should not simply go through the motions, seek recruits from familiar sources and obtain a comfortably adequate crop of young players. How many corporate human resources graduate recruitment departments can boast this attitude?

Clubs with the most ambitious youth policies have gone to great lengths to recruit and retain the best young talent. Don Revie, the great Leeds United manager, built a formidable youth system in the 1960s which was used as a springboard for the club's success in the late 1960s and early 1970s. Syd Owen, the club coach at the time, described his typical day during that era:

❝Harry Reynolds (the chairman) would drive down to the ground at 3.30–4 after training, then we would drive up to Scotland to see the

parents of a boy we were interested in. Nothing was too much trouble. Then we would drive back halfway through the night and had to be down at the ground again at 8.30 for another morning's training.**99**

The signing of Peter Lorimer, whom Leeds had long been chasing, was a further example of Revie's determination to recruit the very best:

66When Revie was tipped off that another club was all set to sign him, he and Maurice Lindley, his assistant, left by car for Scotland at 8 p.m. heading for Dundee. They had to reach Queensferry by 11.30 to catch the final ferry across the Firth of Forth.**99**

Revie takes up the story:

66Ours was the last car on. At the other side we set off again – and I was stopped for speeding as we hurtled through Perth in the middle of the night. Fortunately, the policeman was a football supporter. We arrived at Peter Lorimer's door at 2 a.m., knocked up the whole house and signed him. At 8 a.m. our rivals turned up, only to find they'd been beaten to him.**99**

SUPPLEMENTING THE YOUTH PRODUCTS

Despite the emphasis on recruiting personnel for the long term, short-term needs cannot be neglected. It takes time for young players to be found, then trained and prepared in the way the club requires. In the meantime, life must go on. Bobby Robson started to place great emphasis on youth development soon after his

arrival at Ipswich Town in 1969. The home-grown players found by Robson's team formed the core of the sides which won the FA Cup in 1978 and the UEFA Cup in 1982, great achievements for a relatively small club such as Ipswich. However, before these players broke through, Robson had a job on his hands to retain Ipswich's First Division status. He bought cheaply during this transitional phase, bringing in Frank Clark, Jimmy Robertson, Allan Hunter, Rod Belfitt and David Johnson, and it was their arrival which helped keep Ipswich in the First Division while the young talent came through.

Revie faced a similar position in his early years as Leeds United manager. Languishing in the lower reaches of the Second Division when he took over in March 1961, he urgently needed stop-gap personnel who could keep the ship afloat before the youth system began to reap dividends. As Syd Owen said:

  ❝It was a race against time. To stabilize the position, we had to get some mature professional players ... Bobby Collins, Freddie Goodwin, Willie Bell. They were reliable, honest players ... Don knew they would help the club until we had four or five years to get the Jimmy Greenhoffs and the Norman Hunters through.❞

Leeds narrowly escaped relegation in 1961 and 1962, finished fifth in 1963 and were Second Division champions in 1964.

A productive youth policy, however, can have its drawbacks. If a group of players reach the first team, establish themselves and achieve success, then younger players coming through will find it more difficult to obtain the necessary experience to further their careers, as their way has been blocked.

This has indeed been the case for many young hopefuls at Manchester United in the past few years. Ferguson stresses that the club does not make hasty decisions about young talent: 'We do well with them here because anybody who comes knows that if they are good enough they will get a chance. We are patient. We don't discard too easily. We prefer to let players develop.' Despite the club's patience, a string of players – John Curtis, Danny Higginbotham, Alex Notman, Michael Appleton, Jonathan Macken and David Healy, to name but a few – have been released by United to pursue careers of varying degrees of success at other clubs. Only a real exceptional talent such as Wes Brown, who is now a regular member of the first-team squad, can hope to break through in the face of such competition.

> A productive youth policy, however, can have its drawbacks.

This situation can provide a disincentive to young players to join the club and can eventually lead to stagnation and complacency. This can in turn lead to a deterioration of the club's fortunes, thus breaking the cycle of self-perpetuating success. It is therefore necessary periodically to recruit top-class experienced players to provide the necessary internal competition and help to maintain a consistent level of performance.

Nevertheless, football has consistently demonstrated the benefits of an emphasis on recruitment of players who are starting their careers. Together with the advantages discussed above, it saves the significant expenditure on transfer fees and salaries in signing established stars. But perhaps the main long-term benefit might be the cultivation of a close bond and team spirit among the young players which serves to increase the club's chances of success when some of these players go on to form the nucleus of the senior team in years to come. As Ferguson says: 'There's no doubt that the youngsters are the heart of the team. They create the team spirit, the ethic, the core of experience. They create the soul of the club.'

Lesson

```
Companies, like football teams, must see
the 'marathon' not just the 'sprint'.
While  continuing  to  compete  in  the
sprint they must manage the expectations
of  their  stakeholders  based  on  their
knowledge of the marathon.
```

The management team – who does what?

IN FEBRUARY 2001, CHARLES ALLEN BECAME CHAIRMAN OF THE GRANADA Group, which comprises London Weekend Television, Anglia, Yorkshire TV, Tyne Tees TV, Meridian and, of course, Granada TV. His promotion marked the end for Allen of more than a decade as loyal lieutenant to Gerry Robinson. One of the most infamous and successful double-acts in modern corporate history had come to an end.

Allen first met Robinson at Grand Metropolitan, the food and entertainment company, in the mid-1980s. Together, they masterminded the management buy-out of Compass, the catering group, from GrandMet. Robinson became chief executive and Allen was appointed managing director. In 1991, Robinson was handed the task of turning round the troubled Granada Group. He had big plans for Granada and sought out his trusted number two to assist him in the company's restructuring.

The subsequent years saw Granada undertake a series of astute acquisitions within the television and hospitality industries, including the famous hostile takeover of Forte Group in 1996. The strategy of Robinson and Allen was eventually to make both the television and the hospitality sides of the business independently powerful enough to be split into separately quoted companies. The final piece in the jigsaw enabled them to achieve their goal. They went back to their old hunting ground and snapped up Compass for £6 billion. The hospitality side of the business was promptly demerged, Robinson stepped aside to become a non-executive director and handed his crown to Allen, who became chairman of the new media company.

The partnership had brought great financial success. In the year they took over, Granada posted a loss of £110 million. Within five years, Granada was the best-performing stock in the FTSE-100 index and Robinson and Allen had become the darlings of the City.

The secret of the partnership lay in the way they complemented each other so perfectly. Robinson was the front man, with a shrewd eye for the bigger picture and the Irish charm to convince others that his chosen course was the correct one. At one City stockbroker they even nicknamed him 'the Fairground Hypnotist' as his talk and manner were so persuasive. As one analyst said: 'It is the way he draws you in, and then the voice lowers, and it is like you are sinking into a hypnosis. We have this joke that one day in a Granada meeting we will all come to with a jolt and find we have taken half our clothes off or something.'

> Robinson and Allen had become the darlings of the City.

However, complementarity is nothing unless the senior partner is brave enough to make the most of the situation by delegating, to his junior partner, responsibility for those tasks at which the junior partner excels. Robinson was a master of such delegation. He asserts that he never got involved in detail when it was not necessary:

"Everyone always thinks groups like Granada are run from the top. They can't be. Personally when I was a junior I always hated having to explain the detail of what I was doing to someone else. Providing you deliver the thing at the end of the day, you like to be left alone. Most people I know manage things like that."

But here Robinson was being disingenuous. He was aware that top management needed to keep a grip on the detail of the company, but he also knew that he was not the man best suited to this task. What he did recognize was that Charles Allen *was* suited to the task.

Robinson said of his former partner: 'He has got this extraordinary combination of a capacity to see the big picture and implement the detail, and that is a very unusual combination.' A typical example of Allen's concern for the minutiae of the business came soon after the Forte takeover. Productivity in hotel housekeeping was transformed by a thorough overhaul of the previous Forte systems under which housekeepers were paid a standard rate no matter what size the room. As Allen said: 'The longer it took them to do the room, the better.' Allen introduced a system whereby staff were paid according to which type of room they serviced. The new method not only incentivized staff – 'Once they finish, they can go,' Allen said – but also enabled hotels to prioritize the check-out rooms and improve turnaround times.

Maybe Gerry Robinson had been studying his football history before he aligned himself so closely to Allen. As we shall see later, the Robinson and Allen partnership, as well as others like Archie Norman and Allan Leighton at Asda, Hewlett and Packard themselves, and Lord Hanson and Lord White, bore a striking resemblance to those of well-known football management duos, such as Shankly and Paisley, Mercer and Allison, Ferguson and Kidd and subsequently, Ferguson and McLaren.

These partnerships all demonstrated the value of having a front-man at the helm, being the public face of the organization, the strategic thinker and the natural motivator. Behind the scenes, the other partner is the detail man, or as Allen was once described, 'the urgent, hard-driving executor: the ultimate deliverer'. Both Allen and McLaren, who was appointed as manager of Middlesbrough in June 2001, now have the chance to emulate Paisley and make a name for themselves as the top man in their organization. Football tells us that their performance will be affected greatly by the choices they, in turn, make in selecting their own management team.

So what exactly can football tell us about the issue of delegation? What should the head of an organization or a department look for in an assistant or a supporting management team? Should he choose people he knows and feels comfortable with? Should he work side by side with a joint manager, someone to share the onerous responsibilities of leadership equally with him? Should a newly appointed manager retain a direct involvement in the business in which he was previously involved? Or should he delegate this work and concentrate solely on ensuring that the organization or team is running efficiently and on managing others so that they perform to the best of their ability?

PLAYERS TO MANAGERS

In business, managers are invariably promoted because they are good at their job – that is, they are good accountants or good lawyers. However, as football has shown us, there is no reason why functional expertise and managerial competence should be in any way related. The mistaken belief that they *are* related leads to many poor appointments, both in football and in business.

There are other reasons why promoting the most able functional performer might potentially be misguided. First, some managers are prevented from doing what they are good at and made to do something for which they have little aptitude and no relevant experience. Imagine, for example, making David Beckham non-playing manager of Manchester United. This would clearly not be a wise move for the club at the present moment since Beckham adds enormous value to the front-line. Moving him would, therefore, damage the core business.

> Some managers are prevented from doing what they are good at and made to do something for which they have little aptitude and no relevant experience.

Second, many newly promoted managers with developed functional ability still want to continue what they were previously doing so well, even when they are burdened with the additional responsibilities of management. In football this is clearly visible and manifests itself in the player–manager syndrome. In business it is less obvious but just as unsatisfactory – it is rarely the most productive use of the individual's time.

The promoted managers might prefer continuing in a functional role because they do not trust others to do that functional job as well as they could. Alternatively, it might be because their remuneration is still connected in some way to personal business production or sales, in addition to the performance of their team or department under their management. Or it might simply be that they want to carry on doing something which they are good at and feel comfortable with as it gives them enjoyment, satisfaction and a sense of self-worth. After all, enjoying a job helps make a person more dedicated to it and possibly more proficient at it, and such commitment will have made that person promotion material in the first place.

The difficulty is that it is simply not possible to do two such diverse jobs simultaneously. The strains placed on the performance by unrealistic expectations will damage the chances of success in *both* roles. Managers would be better served delegating all their functional work, concentrating solely on recruiting the right people and on ensuring that the staff under their management are motivated and working together, as a cohesive unit, towards the attainment of a defined strategic goal. That is their task.

Notwithstanding our view that player–managers are bad for your corporate health, they continue to exist in football. Examination of some instances where it has occurred may help with a final judgement.

COMBINING THE ROLES

Playing and managing are generally separate roles in football. Players see out their career and if afterwards they want to manage and some club wants to hire them, they then become a manager. However, there have been many instances in British football in the past 15 years when a player has been appointed as manager prior to the end of his career, before eventually scaling down the playing aspect of his job and concentrating solely on being a manager.

This concept of the player–manager became a popular concept only in the 1980s. It has never been viewed as an ideal arrangement but as a necessary, pragmatic compromise. Player–managers have been appointed because an individual has been deemed to be the right man for the job as manager. If that individual is still a good player, then it has been considered best on the balance of things to allow him to continue to perform both roles.

The timing of this proliferation of player–managers was not due to any modern trend of younger managerial appointments. Alf Ramsey, Stan Cullis and Don Revie were all appointed as managers by the time they were 35, and Revie in 1961 was the last of those to become a manager. By the 1980s, however, improved fitness levels and improvement in the treatment of injuries were prolonging players' careers. There was now increasingly an overlap between the time a player reached the necessary maturity to become a manager and his continuing usefulness as a player.

With this development, football began to reflect practice in the business world where people often fulfil both functional and managerial roles. How then have these player–managers fared? The answer, as is perhaps inevitable for a sample of this size, is very mixed. There have been successes. Examples include Kenny Dalglish who won the League and Cup double for Liverpool in his first season as player–manager in 1985/86. Graeme Souness won the league in Scotland with Glasgow Rangers in his first season in charge in 1986/87. Peter Reid attained impressive league positions for Manchester City as player–manager in the early 1990s. However, there have also been high-profile failures, such as Chris Waddle at Burnley or Terry Butcher at Coventry City and Sunderland.

The conclusions we can draw from this are not clear-cut. Dalglish, Souness and Reid all went on to achieve success in varying degrees after they had hung up their football boots for good.

Waddle and Butcher have not gone back into management since and so we do not know for sure whether it was the combination of the two roles that hindered their eventual progress to be great managers or whether they simply lacked the necessary attributes in the first place. What is interesting, however, is the overall trend during the past few years. There are still a number of player–managers employed by the 92 league clubs, but there are interestingly no longer any in the Premiership and have been none since the then Chelsea manager Gianluca Vialli retired as a player in the summer of 1999.

It seems that there has been a subtle shift in the balance of attitudes towards player–managers. The player–manager concept, previously viewed as imperfect but tolerable, is now believed to be something which should be avoided if at all possible, especially in the highly pressurized atmosphere of the Premiership. How else can we explain the fact that Vialli himself, a world-class striker and at 34 still then with much to offer, played only a handful of games for Chelsea in 1998/99? More recently, the French international player Franck Sauzee quit playing immediately upon his elevation to the manager's post at Hibernian when the incumbent manager, Alex McLeish, resigned.

The player–manager concept has been increasingly viewed within football to have several inherent disadvantages. First, if a manager is playing, he is not in a position to view the game from a detached perspective and therefore generally delegates authority for mid-game tactical switches to an assistant. Preventing the manager from exercising tactical judgement is clearly a serious diminution of his role. Even between games, the player–manager's more long-term strategic choices will also potentially suffer from this lack of detachment. Although he can watch video recordings of his team's performance, his strategy will not be informed by the broader and thus more helpful picture afforded by watching them play from the stands, or by being able to observe training sessions without being actively involved.

Stuart Pearce, a player–manager for a few months at Nottingham Forest in 1996/97, argues that being too closely involved with the players also makes it difficult for the player–manager to exercise the necessary impersonal and sometimes ruthless objectivity. When asked if he would ever become a player–manager again, Pearce replied: 'No, I wouldn't do that again. It's just too difficult a job. It's hard when you've got to make decisions about players but they're also your mates as well. It's very hard to be the boss and one of the lads.'

> It's very hard to be the boss and one of the lads.

All the time and effort spent training and playing is also time and effort not spent managing. Moreover, it reduces the player–manager's energy levels and hence his effectiveness when he does turn his mind to management. Talking about his time as player–manager, Graeme Souness said: 'It was difficult. I had to train with the lads and deal with their problems and do all the other work that goes with the job. It was hard to get the rest I needed.' Of course, Souness delegated training and match-day duties to his assistant Walter Smith. When Souness left Rangers he handed the baton to Smith, who in turn delegated duties to *his* coach, Archie Knox.

Not only does the player-manager have to play, there is also the further expectation that he should excel alongside his charges. Jan Molby, player–manager at Swansea City in 1996/97, said: 'As player–manager you have to be the best player on the pitch. There's more pressure.'

Discussion of the drawbacks of the player–manager concept is much further advanced in football than in business, where many managers continue to combine managerial duties with a heavy workload of business tasks. The excuse often given by managers is that they do not want to lose touch or to become removed from developments in the business by not being actively involved. But how removed can they be if every day they are managing, observing and talking to individuals who are still actively involved in the business? When was the last time Alex Ferguson played a professional football match?

Admittedly, some small businesses do not have the luxury of choice. Their managers must often turn their hand to everything if their business is to survive and flourish. Football suggests to those who do have a choice that they ought to consider allowing the players to play and concentrating their own efforts on the management.

JOINT MANAGERS – TWO'S A CROWD

Reed Elsevier, the Anglo-Dutch publisher, decided in 1998 to abandon its unwieldy dual management structure and appoint a single chief executive with a uniform board. The previous system, whereby an English co-chief executive shared control of the company with a Dutch counterpart, had led to five years of damaging political infighting and poor financial performance. Out went Nigel Stapleton and Hernan Bruggink, to be replaced by one man, Crispin Davies. Similarly, Sandy Weill and John Reed lasted only 18 months as Citigroup's top team, and Jurgen Schrempp and Bob Eaton failed to work together when Daimler acquired Chrysler. Could any of these joint management structures have worked? The experience of football indicates that the chances of success were minimal from the outset.

The 1987 FA Cup Final was unique for two reasons. Coventry City won the trophy for the only time in their history. And John Sillett and George Curtis thereby became the only joint managers in English football history to achieve any real success. In September 2000, Millwall sacked their joint managers Keith Stevens and Alan McLeary after two years at the helm. They were the latest club to experiment unsuccessfully with joint managers. Charlton Athletic, whose current manager Alan Curbishley originally shared the post with Steve Gritt, and Liverpool, who originally appointed Gerard Houllier to work with Roy Evans, both sacked one of the pair and found considerable success with the other. Millwall took the step of dispensing with both. As at Charlton and Liverpool, the Millwall board's decision was rewarded handsomely. Their chosen replacement, Mark McGhee, acting as sole manager, duly won the Division Two championship for the club at the end of the same season.

The appointment of joint management duos at Charlton and Liverpool were both the result of a lack of decisiveness by the respective boards. In the summer of 1991, Gritt and Curbishley applied separately for the vacant manager's position at the club. Both were prepared to work as assistant to whomever got the job. The board, unable to differentiate between the two, appointed them jointly.

The club finished in mid-table in the First Division for the four seasons in which Gritt and Curbishley were in joint control. By the end of the 1994/95 season the board sensed that the arrangement was not bearing fruit in the way it had hoped. It did not believe that either was a bad manager, simply that the concept of a joint management pairing was not working in practice. Gritt was the unlucky one, as he recalls: 'I couldn't do anything about it as it was just a change of club policy when Charlton decided to go with one manager out of the two of us ... and they chose Curbs.' Curbishley has since led Charlton to two promotions, and in the 2000/01 season, the club finished a highly creditable ninth in the Premiership, equalling their best-ever performance.

Liverpool's appointment of Gerard Houllier as joint manager with Roy Evans in July 1998 was an ill-conceived fudge. The board had clearly decided that Evans's performance as manager over four seasons was not satisfactory – otherwise, they would not have been seeking another manager. But Evans was part of the fabric of the club. He had been there for 33 years as a player, coach, a respected member of the famous 'Boot Room' (as we shall see later, the very embodiment of the soul of the club) and finally as the manager. The board simply lacked the heart to sack him outright. Dismissing him would be to sever a bond with the glorious years of success which anyone connected with Liverpool looked back on with great fondness.

Another related reason for the board's fudge was that it was wary of change. It had not appointed a complete outsider since Bill Shankly had taken over in 1959 and continuity had served it well for three decades. The joint appointment was thus an expression of the board's confusion. It strongly suspected that an outside appointment was necessary, but sacking and replacing Evans immediately would have meant too sudden and harsh abandonment of the club's management ethos.

> Another related reason for the board's fudge was that it was wary of change.

Wittingly or otherwise, by appointing Houllier alongside Evans, the board did ensure that Evans's tenure was doomed, but that the transition would be more gradual. The official line was that the managers would work in tandem and if they encountered problems they would resolve them together. However, as one observer put it: 'The reality, as everyone saw it, was that any improvement in performance would be viewed as evidence of Houllier's ability, and any worsening of the situation would be an indictment of Evans's work at the club.' In November, four months after the joint appointment, with the team suffering poor results, Evans left the club 'by mutual consent'.

Houllier's comments after Evans's departure reveal why joint management arrangements are unworkable in practice: 'I feel very sorry over Roy's departure as I really liked working with him and our relationship was always fine. The joint manager situation was more of a problem for the players, staff and media.' He said subsequently: 'I regret Roy's decision but at the same time I understand it … It was difficult for the players in the long run, the players like to be able to refer to one manager. The concept was obviously extremely difficult for them.'

The joint management arrangement might not have been a problem for Houllier, but this was irrelevant. He was not being managed. The important issue, which Houllier accepted, was that the players and staff felt more comfortable with one focus of authority. It is easy to understand why. Whose instructions should they listen to? Who should they approach with a problem? Authority was diffused. The players craved the sense of security and purpose derived from working for one manager who possesses a clear and credible vision and the drive to implement it. Under Houllier's sole management, the club's fortunes have improved steadily, culminating in the capture of three major trophies in 2001.

Similar examples exist in the biggest of businesses. In July 2001, for example, William Clayton Ford III, chairman of the Ford

Motor Corporation, suddenly announced the creation of an 'office of the chairman and CEO'. That CEO, Australian Jacques 'Jac' Nasser, was happy, the world was told, with a statement by Ford which asserted that 'this new structure allows both Jacques and me to work hand in hand to lead the company'. The story was that the change was merely a formalization of the arrangement that already existed between the two. It was *not*, the company argued, a replay of the situation in the 1970s when Harry Ford II instituted a three-man 'office of the chief executive' before ousting president Lee Iacocca.

They were partially right – Iacocca lasted a year after the reorganization, Nasser lasted only three months. Nasser effectively ignored the change in structure and continued to act in the autocratic manner that had precipitated the change in the first place. When called into the chairman's office on the morning of 28 October 2001, Nasser is reported to have opened the conversation with the line: 'So, you're going to fire me, are you?' Ford's reply is not recorded but Nasser left the same morning. Perhaps Nasser was a student of the Premier League and knew what was coming, whether or not he changed his ways. His stubbornness only accelerated the inevitable.

Even if kindred spirits are found, the joint management option is surely flawed in the long term. Resentments and friction will inevitably build up between the two – 'I am doing more work than him and he is getting half the credit.' 'If only he agreed with me on this issue, we wouldn't be in such a mess.' 'Why's he getting the same money as me when I am making all the decisions?' Moreover, as the experience of the Houllier/Evans partnership testifies, any poor short-term performance leads to a suspicion that it is the joint management arrangement that is not working, whether in reality the two are connected or not. The uncertainty over the managers' future reduces their authority with the players and builds the immediate pressure which prevents them from the gradual building of the foundations for long-term success.

The failure of joint managers raises a crucial issue about matrix management in business. In most reasonably complex corporate organizations there is some sort of matrix structure – classically geographic and functional. Therefore, many of the staff report to two managers, their geographic head and their functional head. Football suggests that the opportunity to appeal to two bosses is an opportunity to avoid responsibility.

What happened to Sillett and Curtis? Despite their success in their one season together, Curtis stood down and Sillett assumed sole command. Would Curtis have won the Cup and then immediately stood down if he had been sole manager?

THE MANAGEMENT TEAM

One identifiable person might need to have ultimate responsibility and authority, but that person cannot operate single-handedly. There have been several examples in recent years of business leaders whose style has been criticized as overly autocratic and resistant to constructive advice. Stitched on a cushion in former Marks and Spencer chief Sir Richard Greenbury's office were the words: 'I have many faults, but being wrong is not of them.' These words were later to prove to be an ironic reflection on his failure to accept quickly enough the necessity for a radical change in strategy. Greenbury should have learned more from his avowed managerial hero, Alex Ferguson. Peter White, who once said his board was only 'fit to visit the Chelsea Flower Show', was deposed as chief executive of Alliance & Leicester in 1999 after the board claimed that it could no longer stand his autocratic style, insisting 'a more consensual style of leadership is needed'. Is there anything football can tell us about the benefits of encouraging an active contribution from the management support team?

The first thing Joe Mercer did when he was offered the post as Manchester City manager in the summer of 1965 was to appoint Malcolm Allison as his assistant. It was an inspired move. The previous season, City had finished 11th in the Second Division. Within five years, the partnership had captured the League Cham-pionship, the FA Cup and the European Cup Winners Cup.

'I have many faults, but being wrong is not one of them.'

The success of the partnership confirmed Mercer's belief that management should not be a lonely pursuit: 'As far as I'm concerned, managing is a team game. A good manager, a good number two and a good chairman ... It's a combination of things as far as I'm concerned. Nobody does it on their own.'

The great football managers have always understood the value of an able assistant and a strong support team. Herbert Chapman, the first of the great British managers, said of his right-hand man, Tom Whittaker: 'If trainers were transferred like players, his fee would be beyond price.' Since Chapman's day, several management duos have earned their place in football folklore. Their names have become automatically intertwined in the mind of the football fan – Shankly and Paisley, Busby and Murphy, Clough and Taylor, Mercer and Allison.

What lessons then can football teach business managers in how to go about selecting the support team? The first point to make is that insecurity should not play a part in the decision-making process of the talented and self-confident manager. As Jimmy Armfield says, many lesser managers in football have fallen into the trap of appointing people because they know them well and do not feel threatened by them, and not necessarily because they are the best possible candidates:

66I've always felt managers don't try to obtain the best staff. It suggests to me that there's a degree of insecurity within them. And yet they have a responsibility to their clubs. If they are ill, who will take over? You should have the best staff you can find.99

Jim McGregor, formerly a physiotherapist at Manchester United, agrees:

66Managers like to feel secure. This is why, increasingly these days, the new manager brings in his own team. Even the medical man is at risk. That used to be unheard of – he was part of the bricks and mortar. But when a new manager comes in now, the entire backroom staff shake in their shoes.99

As we have seen, self-belief is one of the hallmarks of the great manager. Bill Shankly was certainly not one to suffer from insecurity. He was confident enough in his ideas and ability to give the incumbent management team a chance when he first arrived at Liverpool in 1959. Bob Paisley, Joe Fagan and Reuben Bennett, who were all to go on to become vital members of the management team in the Shankly era, had all presumed the sack. But Shankly assured them: 'I'm not bringing in my own men. I'm keeping you all on as long as you guarantee me just one thing – utter loyalty, loyalty to each other and loyalty to Liverpool FC.'

Alex Ferguson has learned over the years that much time and effort needs to be devoted to finding the right people to join the management team, such is the importance of the decision. Indeed, his increasing self-confidence and maturity as manager of Manchester United can be measured by the amount of thought he has put into this selection process. On taking over in 1986, he simply brought in his trusted assistant from his Aberdeen days, Archie Knox, as his number two. But when Knox's eventual replacement Brian Kidd resigned in December 1998, it took Ferguson two months of painstaking research before he finally found the type of assistant he believed he now needed, in the shape of the little-known Steve McLaren, then assistant manager at Derby County. In his autobiography, Ferguson wrote: 'I instructed Eric Harrison, our former youth coach, and Les Kershaw, director of the Academy, to scour England for the best candidates in terms of coaching ability and work ethic. Their researches kept coming back to Steve.' Arguably, United's chaotic start to the 2001/02 season was in large part due to his failure to appoint a replacement for McLaren.

Ferguson also came to the conclusion that the club needed a technical coach who could work on the skills of the younger players and teach the other coaches how to develop the skill levels of all players. The introduction of this new role, Ferguson believed, would bring the standard of coaching methods into line with other major European clubs. The right man was eventually identified. Rene Meulensteen, a Dutchman virtually unknown in English football circles and at the time working in Qatar, was recruited in May 2001.

McLaren and Meulensteen were not Ferguson's friends. It is doubtful whether he had even met Meulensteen before he started talking to him about a possible position at United. But he had carefully thought through the type of skills and experience he needed for the respective roles and had then made sure that he sought out the best man for the job.

Contrast this method with Bryan Robson's selection process at Middlesbrough, which was probably little different from that employed by many managers, both in football and in business. He appointed Viv Anderson as his assistant and Gordon McQueen as his first-team coach, both of whom had been Robson's team-mates when he was a player at Manchester United.

They both might have been good at their jobs. But the suspicion remains that Robson did not look hard enough for the *best* people and instead settled for those he happened to know. This suspicion was reinforced in late 2000 when the Middlesbrough board decided that the team's poor position in the league demanded the addition of the experienced coaching skills of Terry Venables. Venables proceeded to reorganize the team tactically and the club managed to avoid relegation at the end of the season. Robson and his management team, their authority and status severely undermined by what was perceived to be Venables's success, left the club soon afterwards.

> But the suspicion remains that Robson did not look hard enough for the *best* people and instead settled for those he happened to know.

CORRECTING MISTAKES

The inability to remove the wrong people once in place is as big an impediment to success as selecting the wrong people, both in the management team and within the staff, in the first place. There are a variety of reasons for this phenomenon that need to be both recognized and resisted:

➡ First is *wish fulfilment*. Managers or CEOs will often be unable to come to terms with the fact that someone they have selected or promoted is proving to be inadequate. There can be an emotional attachment to someone you have selected. Not so for Ferguson in the case of Jaap Stam who was unceremoniously removed within a week.

➡ Second is *blind loyalty*. The kind of loyalty demonstrated by the Middlesbrough chairman Steve Gibson towards Bryan Robson had the same feel as that of the ill-fated General Motors (GM) pair of Robert Stempel (chairman and CEO) and Lloyd Reuss (president). Stempel was often quoted as referring to Reuss as 'my guy'. Reuss presided over GM's historic losses and eventually both were fired. The loyalty was admirable but impractical. The company acted in its own best interests, just as Gibson at Middlesbrough was eventually forced to do.

➡ Third is *fear of change*. The 'devil-you-know' syndrome. This can often be rationalized on cultural grounds – that an outsider would not understand the culture. In a failing team this might be good.

➡ Fourth is the *'George Best' syndrome*. This is the fatal flaw that all but the very best managers suffer from – the belief that you can coach the player who has been uncoachable by everyone else. It is the classic managerial vanity. How else can the careers of players like Best and other troublesome players like Stan Bowles, Stan Collymore *et al.* be explained?

A lesson we have seen from football is that any decision on recruiting management support should be carefully thought through and ought not to be motivated by insecurity or friendship. However, if that is what *not* to do, what exactly should a manager be looking for in his prospective lieutenants?

SPECIALISTS

Clearly, the candidate must have the specialist expertise relevant to the position. Few people would make a good manager, but many others have a passion or skill which can contribute greatly to the success of an organization. Manchester United's dominance over the past few years has been built to a large degree on finding and then grooming high-quality young players. The man largely responsible for this is the little-known Eric Harrison, United youth-team coach during the maturation of Beckham, Giggs, Scholes, Butt and Neville. His enthusiasm and the satisfaction he has derived from his particular role in the United success story are obvious:

❝It's fantastic to see them now, superstars in the first team. It's something money can't buy. If you are a youth-team coach or manager for a long period of time, you are never going to get rich – even at Manchester United. But I've got something that a lot of other people – managers, assistant managers and first-team coaches – up and down the country have never had.❞

The specialist expertise and personality attributes of the chosen support team should ideally complement those of the manager. David Platt, appointed in July 2001 by Sven Goran Eriksson to manage the England Under-21 team, describes his own selection procedure while manager of Nottingham Forest:

❝In searching for them I had to look at what my weaknesses were and whether their strengths could paper over those weaknesses. And look at their weaknesses and see whether my strengths could compensate. So we've got a circle of staff that provides everything but not one of us is every component of that circle.❞

A developed self-awareness on the part of the manager is therefore crucial if he is to find the most suitable support. He must be prepared to accept that he has shortcomings and be able to identify what they are.

Several of the great partnerships of manager and assistant manager provide us with excellent examples of Platt's concept of the complementary relationship. Francis Lee, a Manchester City player in the late 1960s and early 1970s, describes how the experienced, wise Joe Mercer was the perfect foil for the brilliant but sometimes arrogant and tactless coach, Malcolm Allison:

❝I think it was the perfect combination. Malcolm was probably the best coach I've worked with in football and he motivated the players and got them going and thinking, while Joe was the father figure, pouring oil on troubled waters every time Malcolm stirred up problems ... or caused them.❞

Peter Taylor was Brian Clough's assistant during his highly successful periods as manager of Derby County and Nottingham Forest. Taylor said: 'We just gelled together, we filled in the gaps ... My strength was buying and selecting the right player, then Brian's man management would shape the player.' Most of Clough's astute signings were a result of Taylor's keen eye for potential and he recognized his assistant's contribution: 'The chemistry was absolutely brilliant. He saw things 24 hours earlier than I did regarding players, he was second to none at that.' Clough's teams never achieved the same level of performance after Taylor retired as his assistant in May 1982.

After Brian Kidd left Manchester United in 1998, Alex Ferguson concluded that he needed a replacement who could challenge

United's group of talented players to achieve a yet higher level of accomplishment. Ferguson himself could always be relied upon to recruit wisely, to motivate and inspire the players, to develop a coherent long-term strategy and to oversee the implementation of that strategy. Steve McLaren's dedicated and innovative approach to the detail of the more immediate technical and psychological aspects of team performance made him the perfect foil.

McLaren's whole coaching philosophy is based on the constant striving for individual and collective excellence and the rejection of complacency. This applies even to himself. Few coaches have analyzed the psychology of winning as deeply as McLaren. He cites books written by American professional coaches Pat Riley and Bill Walsh as having had a major impact on his coaching career. He has also studied videos and read transcripts of interviews with Michael Jordan, the greatest modern-day basketball player, and studied the coaching techniques employed by his team, the Chicago Bulls. His library on his specialist subject of winning is apparently still growing.

> Few coaches have analyzed the psychology of winning as deeply as McLaren.

McLaren evaluated and communicated with each senior player at United on a daily basis. He plotted in detail every development in their activity and performance level and then provided feedback to them both individually and collectively. Hard work and planning were key to his method: 'Failure to prepare is preparing to fail' is one of his catch phrases. Under McLaren's diligent and rigorous tutelage, the United team improved still further on their pre-1998 performance – they won an unprecedented Treble in 1999 and won a hat-trick of League Championships before he departed in the summer of 2001.

The relationship of Bill Shankly and Bob Paisley was very similar to that of Ferguson and McLaren. As former player Ian Callaghan says:

66They were the perfect double act. Shanks was the motivator supreme. There was nobody better. Bob's tactical knowledge and of the game generally was incredible. He could watch a match and recognize the qualities of every single player, spotting their strengths and weaknesses.99

Shankly, like Ferguson, was the inspirational figurehead who conceived the long-term strategy which built the foundations for sustained success. Paisley's natural inclination to focus on detail was an ideal complement. He kept a logbook which included all sorts of information about the players:

66I observe training, watch movement, jot down any injuries, anything at all that may be relevant. Everything that could possibly affect a player's performance is entered in the book, no matter how unimportant it may seem. If a player has a birth or death in the family, it goes in the book. So do all the details of weights, injuries, performances and weather conditions, both in training sessions and in matches.99

He also wrote:

66In some cases you can see from the book that a player has good and bad spells of form at the same stage of each season ... Sometimes it enables you to nip problems in the bud ... The slightest scrap of information is worth entering in the log. You never know when it might throw a light on something.**"**

But Liverpool's success could not be attributed just to Shankly and Paisley. One of Shankly's great strengths was the way he unashamedly exploited the full extent of the creative energy of all his management team. 'The Boot Room', so called because this was where the management team used to meet to discuss their ideas, became an intimidating symbol of Liverpool's ceaseless quest for the recipe for perfection.

The Boot Room included Paisley, training staff Joe Fagan, Ronnie Moran and Reuben Bennett, youth development officer Tom Saunders, youth coach John Bennison and chief scout Geoff Twentyman, eventually supplemented by coach Roy Evans. Saunders recalls that they all:

"... used to come into the Boot Room on Sundays and talk about the matches we'd been involved with, but he (Shankly) didn't come in. He knew it was good to let us exchange ideas and thrash it out without him there ... he was using his men superbly well, never playing one off against another. He got the most out of that team.**"**

Shankly had formulated the broad strategy. The Boot Room was filled by those who shared his fundamental vision but who could assist him in the formulation of the necessary detail within the limits of this vision. As Tommy Docherty said: 'He had a team in the Boot Room, men who were disciples of his way and who saw the sense of building from within.'

SOUNDING BOARD/BUFFER/CONDUIT

The great managers have sought to maintain a certain distance from the players, a policy which has preserved their natural authority (see Chapter 3). However, in removing themselves from close contact there is always the chance that they could lose touch with the general mood of the team and the sentiments being expressed by individuals. This possibility clearly has its dangers. If this situation is left unchecked and potential problems are not addressed quickly and decisively, initial dissatisfaction can soon fester and grow into widespread disharmony.

It is vital, therefore, that other members of the management team act as a sounding board for the players and the manager. That role also allows them to be the conduit for concerns between the manager and players. As a consequence the manager will be able to nip incipient problems in the bud. Many assistant managers are well known for performing this role. For instance, players regarded Sean Fallon and Jimmy Murphy, assistants to Jock Stein and Matt Busby respectively, to be far more approachable than their more aloof managers were. Sven Goran Eriksson is one of many managers who have seen the benefits of this kind of arrangement:

66The easiest time to make contact with the players was after the training sessions, when they looked forward to hearing my comments and ideas. But if they needed to talk, the players also tended to prefer going to the assistant coach or the physio, or someone else who didn't bear responsibility for the selection of the team. Even if they didn't talk to me, they hoped the message would reach me.99

In talent-driven businesses (e.g. finance, professional services, consultancy) it is similarly extremely important that management know what is bothering the staff and that managers are assessed by their staff as well as by their superiors. Most businesses pay lip service to 360-degree feedback, but they would do better to think more seriously about its value.

A player's relationship with the manager is crucial. If that breaks down, the player is unlikely to be sufficiently motivated to perform to his full potential. Assistant managers have, therefore, often also viewed it as part of their role to defuse player anger before it causes a heated argument and an irrevocable split with the manager. Bob Paisley was very active in this regard:

A player's relationship with the manager is crucial.

❝Those few yards between the dressing-room and the manager's office are vital. Once a player gets in there, it's an argument. When Bill was manager, I rated a big part of my job as cutting things off before they reached his office. If I could sort out his beef, all well and good. If I couldn't, at least I could offer him some advice, even if was just to delay things and take the heat out of the situation.❞

Complementarity is clearly the watchword for the selection of the senior management team. However, there is continued and serious debate about the credentials of the number two, in particular. Walter Smith, for example, feels that the second-in-command should have had managerial experience himself, albeit often at a lower level. 'I feel that such a man can empathize with your problems and will therefore tend not to second guess your decision;

he knows the score,' said Smith. This view fits with that which says that a number two should be able to step into the breach at a moment's notice. The evidence of consummate number twos like Brian Kidd and Ray Harford (assistant to Kenny Dalglish at Blackburn Rovers during the early 1990s), who have failed to impress as the number one, suggest such qualities may not be necessary.

The approach of using a specialist number two accords with management theories which suggest an outward-looking number one complemented by an inward-looking number two – the chairman and the CEO being separate jobs or even the German model of a supervision board and a management board. However, notwithstanding the structure, the key lesson from football for business managers concerned with issues of delegation is still to ignore any feelings of insecurity. The number two position is clearly so important that only the very best must be selected – and that is a rule for both football and business.

The issues of, and solutions to, managerial failure in business perfectly mirror those in the football world. Why do CEOs fail? Primarily because they fail to put the right people in the right job. Pick the right players to play the right system and you increase the chances of continued success. It may not be rocket science but it is clearly difficult for organizations to grasp the simple fact that *selection* is key.

Lesson

→ Players play and managers manage – make sure roles are defined and add value.

→ Horses for courses – make sure specialists concentrate on their specialisms.

→ Ensure that you select complementary talents.

SEVEN

Creating the team

MERRILL LYNCH WAS QUICK TO APPRECIATE THE OPPORTUNITIES OFFERED BY the merging of two competitors. Soon after Deutsche Bank bought Bankers' Trust in late 1998, Merrill capitalized on the inevitable atmosphere of uncertainty at the new company by snapping up 12 people who had formed the core of what was Bankers' Trust's passive management team. By bringing in this team alongside the incumbent active fund managers, department head Dean D'Onofrio was seeking to retain clients in an increasingly competitive market place. He believed that the quantitative vehicles which the passive management team could establish would bring much-needed variety and appeal to Merrill's product range: 'There is clearly investor demand for these things. We already have $500 million under management and we'd like to keep it there.'

Why did Merrill recruit an entire team from Bankers' Trust? Why did it not just recruit two or three of the key people and then bring in others from elsewhere? Because these individuals were recognized within their particular market as a *team*. By definition a team is greater than the sum of its parts, producing more as a unit than the sum of the potential contributions from each individual member of the team, acting independently. Katzenbach and Smith (1998), experts on the concept of the business team, put it this way:

❝For a real team to form, there must be a team purpose that is distinctive and specific to the small group, and that requires its members to roll up their sleeves and work together to accomplish something beyond individual end-products.**❞**

Indeed, according to Katzenbach and Smith, there is an intangible element which serves to distinguish a genuine team from a mere working group. The latter is really just a set of individuals who interact primarily to share information and to assist each member of the group in handling their area of responsibility more effectively. There is an absence of a shared purpose, goals or a joint product. Real teams, however, are made up of 'a small number of people with complementary skills who are committed to a common purpose, performance goals and approach for which they hold themselves mutually accountable'.

It is this emphasis on the collective pursuit of the common goal which makes a team. Gerard Houllier is one man who is very much aware of this. Sander Westerveld, the former Liverpool goalkeeper, recalls how the players were asked to agree the team's principal target before the start of the 2000/01 season: 'Before the season began we were preparing in Switzerland and everyone wrote down their main aim. Ninety-nine per cent of the players said it was to finish in the top three. We knew how important that was to this club.'

Finishing in the top three in the league would bring qualification to the European Champions League, the most prestigious and lucrative club competition in the world. Liverpool hovered just outside the top three for most of the season in question. Along the way, they happened to win three cup competitions, but the team did not allow these successes to distract them from their agreed primary objective. The competition for third place went to the wire, but their joint resolve gave the team the necessary energy to win six and draw one of their last seven league games and beat off the determined challenges of Leeds and Ipswich.

In a real team, the instinct for individual self-promotion is realized through the pursuit of the team goal. In Katzenbach and Smith's 'high-performance team', each member 'genuinely helps the others to achieve both personal and professional goals'. In other words, individuals actually become committed to one another's personal growth and success.

> In a real team, the instinct for individual self-promotion is realized through the pursuit of the team goal.

Manchester United are a high-performance team. In 1999, they played Juventus in the semi-final of the European Cup. In the first half of the game, their captain Roy Keane was booked and knew therefore that he would be automatically suspended from the final, should United win the tie. Despite the intense personal disappointment he must have felt by potentially missing out on what would have been the most important match of his professional career, Keane thereafter dominated the game, inspiring his team to victory through the sheer force of his performance. Alex Ferguson said of Keane's contribution: 'The minute he was booked and out of the final, he seemed to redouble his efforts to get the team there. He showed that concern for others which separates truly special people.' Ferguson wrote later in his autobiography that 'it was the most emphatic display of selflessness I have seen on a football field'. United had reached such a peak as a team that an individual could set aside any personal emotion to focus all his energies on the achievement of the collective goal.

The manager, despite being outside the team, has a crucial role in its creation and in ensuring that it continues to function as an effective unit. Without Houllier, the Liverpool players would not have formally agreed their goal for the season. Without Ferguson, Keane would not play for Manchester United and the team spirit among the players would not be as strong. But how can a manager produce and maintain this team spirit which creates the 'high-performance team'? How should he go about recruiting individuals for the team? When should he change the team? Let us look at the world of football to find out.

RECRUITING THE TEAM

Just as the manager should ponder long and hard about his choice of his management support, so he should before recruiting people for his operational team.

Martin O'Neill is one example of a top manager who is so concerned with selection that he almost treats his club's money as if it were his own. Tony Balfe, his chairman at Grantham, recalls his parsimony: 'In two years, he spent only £500 and that was after he made several visits to watch the lad. He kept wanting another look and afterwards he was worried that he had spent £500 of the club's money.' At Leicester City, O'Neill studied players like Matt Elliott, Neil Lennon and Muzzy Izzet repeatedly before they were captured. According to Elliott, he never succumbed to exhortations from others to recruit players until he knew he had found the right man: 'Last season, we had a few injuries and people kept putting him under pressure to spend, but he wouldn't. He doesn't dive in and buy players for the sake of it.'

One of the time-consuming elements of recruitment is the task of researching the player's character. The great football managers

accept that raw talent is not enough. They have a clear idea of the personality characteristics which, allied to natural ability, will allow the player to achieve.

Herbert Chapman summarized his recruitment philosophy as follows:

&&Employ, without exception, the very best type of player to represent the club ... above all, he must be a gentleman both on and off the field; he must be a clever player who can think out attractive, constructive tactics; and he must be wholeheartedly enthusiastic and keen to make progress in the game.**

Ronnie Moran, a member of the Liverpool management team, says Bill Shankly 'wanted ability, but attitude too. They had to work, he wanted them to be really upset if they lost, to really feel it.' According to former Liverpool player Alan Kennedy, Bob Paisley 'looked beyond what sort of player you were. He looked at the character of the person first.'

Alex Ferguson says that any United player has to have what he describes as 'mental toughness': 'It is an important factor in any player that plays here. They need to be able to handle everything: the media part, the profile, the pressure on them from the support. They need a toughness to survive.' Talking about his 1994 League and FA Cup double-winning team, Ferguson delights in the competitive nature of his players at that time: 'They were winners and in quite a number of cases the other side of the coin was that they were bad losers ... Bruce, Pallister, Keane, Ince, Hughes, Cantona and Schmeichel [all recruited by Ferguson] were capable of causing a row in an empty house.' The sight of Roy Keane in a recent TV programme storming out of a recreational quiz game with his colleagues, on the grounds that his team were getting harder questions, merely emphasizes the point.

In his autobiography, Jaap Stam caused a furore by disclosing that Ferguson broke worldwide football regulations by meeting with him before receiving permission to do so from his club, PSV Eindhoven. For Eindhoven, this added insult to injury. Only months previously, they had spoken out against Ferguson's unauthorized discussions with their player Ruud van Nistelrooy who, like Stam, was later signed by United. But Ferguson was not going to spend the club's money until he had met the players personally and had satisfied himself that they had the necessary personal qualities to play for his team. If it meant breaking some rule, then so be it.

One way of ensuring that the player has these qualities is to recruit someone who has already worked for you and has impressed. This is fraught with less danger than using a similar policy in recruiting a member of the management support team, where it is essential that the manager finds absolutely the right person to complement his own skills and strengths and therefore should not be unduly influenced by familiarity. Martin O'Neill has learned the strategy of recruiting those you already know from his manager at Nottingham Forest, Brian Clough. Clough recruited John McGovern four times, John O'Hare three times and Archie Gemmill twice during his managerial career. Since O'Neill has been at Celtic, he has picked up Neil Lennon and Steve Guppy who were his players during his Leicester days. He also had Guppy with him at Wycombe Wanderers.

Another of O'Neill's ideas is to recruit players who might feel that their talents have not been fully recognized at their current club and are therefore extremely eager to demonstrate their worth. He realizes that one of the most powerful motivating forces is the desire to prove others wrong. Alex Ferguson has noted this approach of O'Neill's: 'He has been a very shrewd buyer of players, and often you will find that he signs up players who have a point to prove. Look at Chris Sutton and Neil Lennon – they are typical Martin signings because they appeared to have been a bit unsettled at their old clubs. In

> One of the most powerful motivating forces is the desire to prove others wrong.

these circumstances, he tends to get that little bit more out of them because they are bursting to do well and prove themselves. These are guys who perhaps felt they were surplus to requirements and here's Martin O'Neill telling them they're brilliant.'

STILL THE RIGHT TEAM?

The manager must review whether his team still has the necessary resources when it is faced by a new, and maybe tougher, challenge. Football tells us that the successful manager is ruthlessly honest with himself about the abilities of the members of the team, and will not hesitate to bring in suitable additions to his squad of players if changing circumstances demand it. When Nottingham Forest scraped promotion to the First Division in 1977, Brian Clough was keenly aware that his team would not be good enough to make an impression in the top division without high-standard reinforcements. Within a month of the start of the new season, he had invested in three players of proven quality – Peter Shilton, Kenny Burns and Archie Gemmill. A few months later, Forest had pulled off the remarkable feat of winning the League Championship in their first season after being promoted.

Clough's recruitment policy in this crucial period can be contrasted with that of Joe Royle after Manchester City's promotion to the Premiership in 2000. City had won two promotions in succession and it should have been clear to Royle that his squad, most of whom had been playing in the Second Division for City a little over a year previously, would struggle to reach a sufficiently high standard of play to ensure survival in the Premiership. City had money to spend and the media hype at the start of the season spotlighting the return of a club with an illustrious past to the top league should have enabled them to attract top-class players. However, Royle failed to invest in the necessary quality, spending £13 million on six players who were arguably of no higher standard than those he already had at his disposal, and the club was punished with immediate relegation.

All teams require frequent rejuvenation. If the team is successful, this should involve planned and incremental redundancies rather than wholesale and dramatic changes. Bob Paisley learned from his predecessor Bill Shankly's mistakes that freshness and competition had to be maintained within his team through regularly recruiting new faces. Alex Ferguson has continued to buy the odd player every season throughout United's successful period, such as Roy Keane in 1993, David May in 1994, Andy Cole in 1995 and Ronnie Johnsen and Ole Gunnar Solskjaer in 1996, in order to reinvigorate the team and avoid the potential for staleness and complacency.

United won the League in 1993 and the League and FA Cup in 1994. In 1995, they won nothing. Ferguson then sold three top players, Hughes, Ince and Kanchelskis, and in the following season the now ripe youngsters he had carefully nurtured (see Chapter 5) played on a much more regular basis, resulting in United winning the League and FA Cup.

Because of his careful recruitment and youth policy, the interregnum at Manchester United had lasted just one year. Again in 1998, United did not win a trophy. Ferguson bought Jaap Stam, Dwight Yorke and Jesper Blomqvist and the team proceeded to win virtually every competition they entered in 1999. The team was constantly being kept on the boil. Once more in 2001, after United had failed to win the European Cup for two years in succession, Ferguson felt his team had become tired and required the boost of a couple of top-quality recruits to spur them on to a higher level. Roy Keane describes the lift which the introduction of Ruud van Nistelrooy and Juan Sebastian Veron gave to the team: 'There's a good feeling about the camp and the two new players have been a big help to everybody. Even in training now there seems to be a bit of extra buzz.'

On this issue, Jack Charlton, the former Republic of Ireland manager, argued for what he called the 'four-year rule'. Every four years either the manager or the players must change. In other words, after a certain period, familiarity really does breed contempt.

THE RECRUITMENT CYCLE

Ferguson has shown that it is not just who you recruit but when you recruit them. Timing is crucial. The experiences of Manchester City in 1972 and Newcastle United in 1996 show that getting this timing wrong can be costly. In March 1972, Manchester City were heading towards the League Championship when their manager, Malcolm Allison, recruited Rodney Marsh from Queens Park Rangers. The team had been functioning efficiently until that point, but the addition of Marsh's unpredictable flair disrupted the team's pattern and cost them the league. The former City player Mike Doyle explains:

❝It was clear Marsh just wanted to do his own thing. You don't win anything with players like that in your side ... All we had to do was to win three games to get the championship. But they persisted in playing Marsh and we lost all our rhythm and everything. We blew it.❞

A similar scenario unfolded after Newcastle had signed Faustino Asprilla, another talented but erratic individualist, in February 1996. Kevin Keegan, the Newcastle manager, had said that he would 'spend £7.5 million on Faustino Asprilla to make sure we win the League Championship'. But by forcing Asprilla into the team, Keegan had merely succeeded in disturbing a winning system. Newcastle threw away a 12-point lead at the top of the table, winning only five of their last thirteen games.

Doyle says that players like Marsh prevent a team from succeeding. That is, someone who may be talented on an individual level but not generally viewed as a team player detracts from the overall performance of the team. This is a view frequently expressed in business where candidates are habitually asked in interviews to cite examples to prove they are a team player and where strongly independent people are often viewed with suspicion by management and other members of the team, even if it is recognized that they have ability.

> In certain circumstances, the perceived maverick can contribute greatly to the success of the team.

So what does football tell us about this issue? Doyle's comments are not atypical. Football (British football anyway) generally feels uncomfortable with the maverick. Ian St John, the former Liverpool player and media personality, reveals why he believes a

player like Frank Worthington, regarded within the game as talented but non-conformist, is a hindrance to a team:

> ❝Frank was a great artist, but I think the sum total of his medals is nil. He couldn't be in a championship-winning team because he was too much of an individualist. There were other brilliant entertainers that I'd like to put in the same bracket. Like everybody else, I loved to see them play, but I was happy they weren't in my team.❞

But the experience of Eric Cantona at Manchester United indicates that in certain circumstances, the perceived maverick can contribute greatly to the success of the team. Cantona had played for numerous clubs before he came to United in 1992. Despite his undoubted ability, no manager wanted to deal with his headstrong and sometimes ill-disciplined character for long, and he would be sold on elsewhere. At Leeds, his last club before joining United, the manager Howard Wilkinson believed that he was not a team player, that he would not fight for the team when things were not going well, and consequently omitted him for many games. Wilkinson could not tolerate Cantona's sulking reaction to being left out and sold him to United. Within a few months, Cantona had inspired United to their first League Championship for 26 years.

If Cantona had been recruited to join a team already on course to achieve its collective goal, he might well have ended up being viewed in the same way as Marsh and Asprilla. But Cantona was not a superfluous addition to a winning team. He was the catalyst which converted a good team into a great one. The other players did not resent his presence. On the contrary, his team-mates, respecting his superior ability, accepted him as the fulcrum of the team and were grateful to him for lifting the club to a higher plane

and for helping them to achieve their collective goal of winning the League Championship. Although Ferguson's canny man management contributed to his motivation and hence his high performance levels (see Chapter 9), this respect from his peers and their desire to learn from him must also have inspired Cantona. Ryan Giggs's comments accurately reflect the views of Cantona's former team-mates at United:

> **❝Everyone learns from Eric. He's a great trainer ... A lot of players, who just used to go home after training sessions, have seen how hard Eric works and they do stay out longer now and practise their technique.❞**

Meredith Belbin, an expert in team-role research, identified nine roles necessary for a successful business team, ranging from the creative, imaginative 'plant' to the disciplined, reliable 'implementer' to the single-minded, self-motivated 'specialist'. While we do not subscribe to the Belbin view that particular individuals will provide particular and separate role requirements for the team, it is clear that each team needs the roles themselves to be provided. It may actually be that certain individuals are able to provide several of the necessary roles. That is why the search for balance has been a key feature of the top football manager's recruitment policy, not just in terms of specialist position on the field of play but also in temperament.

A mix of nationalities, increasingly common in football clubs and in many businesses, can go a long way to providing this necessary mix of characters. Ian St John points to the multi-cultural nature of Shankly's Liverpool team as a contributory factor in its success:

❝The mix was right, of the Scots, the English and the Irish. I always think the English have very good, upright, strong, dedicated professionals ... I think you need the Celts, I think you need the Scots, maybe the Irish, the Welsh, to add that little bit of something else in the mixture. It's like baking a cake.❞

Politically incorrect nowadays, perhaps, but differing cultures do appear to generate differing attitudes. Making sure the mix is correct is a delicate art but one that the modern football, and business, manager must get right.

Much has been written in recent years about the positive influence of the professionalism and high technical ability of foreign footballers on the English game. There certainly seems to be a general consensus that the finely honed technique of many foreign players has rubbed off on their British and Irish counterparts. Domestic players have also become more disciplined and single-minded as athletes as a result of the influx of talent from abroad. Packie Bonner, the former Republic of Ireland goalkeeper, discusses the effect foreign footballers have had on players such as his compatriot and former team-mate Roy Keane:

❝The advent of the foreign player and the foreign coach into the British game has changed the way footballers live their lives. Gone are the days when footballers gorged on hamburgers, steaks and pints of lager. That foreign influence, as big in the players' bar as it is in the dressing-room, has been to the benefit of players like Roy Keane.❞

THE LEADER ON THE PITCH

In business, the manager sets the overall strategy but because he does not have the opportunity or time to oversee everything, he is to a large extent reliant on his team to execute his plans to the best of their ability. This situation is reflected in football. The manager communicates his tactics to the team before a game. After the game has started, he can shout from the touchline, make tactical substitutions and effect more substantial changes in pattern or formation during the half-time break. But in the hurly-burly of the game, the manager will often be powerless to affect certain aspects of team performance, such as the mood and commitment of the players or very short-term positional manoeuvres.

> The manager communicates his tactics to the team before a game.

This is why football managers are very reliant on players (often but not always appointed to the largely ceremonial role of team captain) who can assume leadership during a game by adapting the manager's strategy to short-term situations and in mirroring his determination to succeed. Don Revie extolled the virtues of his leader on the pitch for many years at Leeds United, Billy Bremner:

66 Even the best-laid plans often require some reappraisal out on the park – and that is where a captain like Billy Bremner proved his value. One of his many jobs was to be able to read the situation out there and to adjust the tactics to the situation. 99

He explained:

66 Our pre-match discussion had laid down guidelines for the game, but we had to expect our opponents to formulate plans of their own to stop ours from working smoothly. If our team ran into trouble, Billy had the responsibility of changing or adapting the tactics. 99

The leader not only organizes, he inspires the rest of the team through the power of his performance and his will to win. Sven Goran Eriksson explains the role of his player Sinisa Mihajlovic when he was manager at Lazio:

66 He's almost like a traffic policeman out there, directing everything, with the other players responding to his play. His willpower seems to spread to the rest of the team. Other players that I could mention in this connection are Nesta, Vieri and Simeone. They have this fantastic ability to take the team with them in a positive direction when the going gets tough. 99

The manager is judged by the success of his team. He is therefore completely driven in his pursuit of success. An individual team member, however, might feel that he can get away with less than total commitment. A leader on the pitch who reflects the manager's will to win and inspires his team-mates can help to avert this damaging situation. Alex Ferguson talks admiringly about his current leader on the pitch, Roy Keane:

66 As you develop a team, you try to get your drive and ambition and the playing principles you believe in to enter into their personalities. You hope they will soak up your values, as if through their pores. 99

He specifies:

&&But if you are lucky, you encounter one or two men who are natural mirrors of your commitment, who are such out-and-out winners that you consider it an honour to be compared with them. That's how I see Roy Keane.&&

According to Ferguson, he has had two types of leaders on the pitch during his time at United – the voluble and overtly committed ones such as Keane or Bryan Robson, or the ones who lead by the example of their high level of performance, such as Eric Cantona or the current captain of England, David Beckham:

&&For me, Beckham would come into the Eric Cantona category, a player who leads by example on the field. Cantona had a great presence on the field and was a scorer of important goals. Similarly, David impresses by his example on the field. He never stops running, he plays with supreme confidence, he always tries his hardest and he scores important goals.&&

He points out the difference between the two types:

&&But he's a very different kind of person to, say, Bryan Robson. David is a quiet person. Bryan Robson was more effusive. He had plenty to say on the field and in the dressing room. He was a natural leader in that respect.&&

Anybody who witnessed Beckham's herculean performance in the World Cup qualifier against Greece in October 2001 will have seen his coming of age as an exemplary captain.

There can be more than one leader on the pitch. John Williams argues that the presence of several leaders on the pitch enabled Liverpool's great side of the 1980s to govern itself to a large degree, without any interference from the manager:

❝Much of the leadership and organization essentially came from within the dressing room. Dalglish sorted out the front end of the team, Alan Hansen the back. And (Joe) Fagan would never have presumed to instruct the players how to behave off the field either. That responsibility was left to the senior players.❞

Howard Kendall recalls how the leaders on the pitch in his successful Everton team of the 1980s rallied those around them:

❝I never had to worry about the team's mental attitude. They have sports psychologists coming in today – we didn't need them, we had Gray, Reid, Heath and Ratcliffe, who were so full of confidence and personality that they brought out the character in other younger players.❞

Indeed, having more than one leader on the pitch will prevent over-reliance on a particular individual. During the 1980s, Manchester United and England depended too much on Bryan Robson, nicknamed 'Captain Courageous' for his heroic leadership qualities. Although a great player, he was plagued by injury, and neither club nor country learned to prosper without his galvanizing influence. Sven Goran Eriksson spent a great deal of time trying to convince his Roma team that they could achieve success without their leader on the pitch, Falcao:

“When I was coach at Roma I had a player the whole team was very dependent on: Falcao, from Brazil. Due to an injury, he only had four matches with us during my time at the club. But in the matches he played, Roma were a completely different team. He went around the pitch, pointing and co-ordinating … Without him the players suffered a block. Falcao's presence or absence was decisive in determining how the players felt, and this in turn determined how well they played.”

With Beckham becoming such a fulcrum, Eriksson must have a similar concern for his England team.

Too many leaders, however, will inevitably start to clash with each other. The manager is best advised to strike a balance in his team between leader types and non-leaders. Eriksson points out that 'you can be a good player without being a leader. You need both leader types and non-leaders to get a good team together.' He goes on to say that one of his strategies as a club manager was to recruit 'new players who brought a winning attitude into the team. It was enough to have two or three players who could serve as my instrument when I wanted to change attitudes and thinking in the team.' Will Railo, the sports psychologist who has worked alongside Eriksson for several years, refers to these individuals as the team's 'cultural architects'.

A great leader on the pitch does not necessarily make a great manager.

It should be emphasized here that a great leader on the pitch does not necessarily make a great manager (see Chapter 2). In fact, being good at one might actually preclude being good at the other. The manager should have the necessary intellect to shape and implement a long-term strategy. He must

also have the self-belief to stick with a strategy he believes in, even when others are pressuring him to abandon it. In other words, he must be independent-minded, perhaps even contrary. A leader on the pitch, on the other hand, should not challenge the manager's overall authority but should serve as an instrument of it.

DEVELOPING AND MAINTAINING TEAM SPIRIT

The effective function of team spirit is to elevate the performance of a disparate collection of individuals to that of a cohesive, dedicated unit. George Graham provides the following description:

❝Only a team player who has been involved in a major event can understand the sense of togetherness that sends the dressing-room temperature soaring in the moments before going out for the kick-off. It is an indescribable feeling, but you can almost reach out and touch it. It's a combination of harmony, brotherhood and a desire to do well not only for oneself but for each other. In short, it's team spirit.❞

The connection between a good team spirit and achievement has often been highlighted. Vince Lombardi, the great American football coach, says that 'the difference between mediocrity and greatness is the feeling players have for each other. Most people call it team spirit. When the team is inspired with that special feeling, you know you've got a winning team.'

Great teams are not necessarily made up only of supremely talented individuals. Team spirit enhances collective performance to a level that would often be impossible to predict by simply assessing the individual abilities of each member of the team. The columnist Jim White believes that Liverpool's success in the

1970s and 1980s could not possibly be attributed to the brilliance of every single player within the team:

> **"**There is no question that the one-for-all, all-for-one mentality generated in the Anfield dressing-room was the engine that drove the great team. With players such as Alan Kennedy, John Wark, Sammy Lee and Craig Johnston, nobody could claim this was a collection of top-notch operators in the manner, say, of the current Real Madrid. Every week, they played as an entity greater than the sum of its parts.**"**

Alex Ferguson supports this view:

> **"**In my business, togetherness is not just a nice concept that you can take or leave according to taste. If you don't have it, you are nothing. Selfishness, factionalism, clique-ishness are all death to a football team. As a manager in football, I have never been interested in simply sending out a collection of brilliant individuals. There is no substitute for talent but, on the field, talent without unity of purpose is a hopelessly devalued currency.**"**

In the 1999/2000 and 2000/01 seasons, Manchester United won the League Championship by a wide margin, finishing eighteen and then ten points above second-placed Arsenal. But with exceptional players such as Henry, Bergkamp, Vieira, Keown and others in the Arsenal side, the margin of United's triumphs is not a reflection of any major gulf in the abilities of the constituent members of each team. Indeed, purely in terms of individual talent, several of the Arsenal players were arguably superior to their United counterpart in their respective specialist position.

Writing in January 2001, Hugh McIlvanney attempted to analyze Arsenal's apparent under-achievement in the league:

66At their best, Arsenal can be a nightmare for any opposition, including United, but sustaining cohesion and wholeheartedness throughout 90 minutes is rarely their strong suit these days.99

He added:

66As a highly respected coach observed last week, they will invariably mount an intense, skilful bombardment early in a game, but if it is not swiftly rewarded with goals, the aggressive spirit wanes and opponents will be given the chance to assert themselves in the later stages. Arsenal's form seems to be at the mercy of a complicated interplay of temperaments and moods.99

United, on the other hand, have possessed a collective drive which allows them to attain a high level of performance consistently, not just when the mood takes them. They are known within football as the team which does not know the meaning of defeat. Spurred on by their relentless spirit, they have regularly managed to salvage a game in its dying moments, most famously in the 1999 European Cup Final when they overcame Bayern Munich with two goals in injury time, having been generally outplayed over the course of the game. They have maintained the high standard of their play even in the less high-profile matches when similarly talented teams with an inferior collective drive might be tempted to take their foot off the pedal.

In October 1999, Gianluca Vialli's Chelsea, another team unable to fulfil the potential suggested by an analysis of its constituent parts, defeated United 5–0. This result and performance were proof, if any was needed, of the Chelsea team's high level of ability. During the remainder of the season, however, they lost matches away from home to Sheffield Wednesday, Derby County and Watford, three of the eventual bottom five in the division. United won all three of these fixtures and finished the season a huge 26 points ahead of Chelsea.

How has this powerful collective will, this team spirit, been created at United, or for that matter at Liverpool during the 1970s and 1980s, or within other great football sides? Team spirit is not formed just because all the players like each other and enjoy each other's company. It is something distinct from friendship, as Alan Hansen points out:

❝ Human nature dictates that if you have 16 players, two coaches and a manager, they won't all like each other. But that doesn't matter as long as you can rely on each other. The only way you can do that is by having a great team spirit, so that when you go on to the pitch you have a bond and unity that holds you together. ❞

Dave Bassett presided over the Wimbledon team which climbed three divisions in the 1980s. The Wimbledon side, nicknamed the Crazy Gang, was famed in football for its team spirit, but Bassett claims that the players were not necessarily all bosom pals:

❝ We had a great team spirit, but not all the players got along. Lawrie Sanchez and John Fashanu didn't fancy each other much – they didn't get on at all in fact – but that didn't mean they wouldn't pass to each other or pull together when they were out on the pitch. ❞

A productive youth system plays a major part in the formation of this team spirit. The better the youth system, the better the young players, the more likely they are to be introduced en masse into the senior team, having already played together for years and having had the opportunity to foster a close camaraderie. The team spirit which differentiated Liverpool and United from their rivals was thus largely derived from both clubs' emphasis on the development of youth.

A large proportion of the young players whom Shankly and Ferguson introduced were from the local area. By filling a significant part of the team with local players, who felt an attachment to the club and were aware of its traditions, they sought to build a club identity which transcended the contribution of any one individual. Geoff Twentyman recalls that Liverpool 'concentrated on Lancashire and other places nearby and we picked up Alec Lindsay and Steve Heighway. Bill wanted locally based lads and even fellas like Clemence and Keegan weren't from too far away.'

Phil Thompson (also brought in by Shankly), who as a boy was an avid Liverpool fan, went on to captain one of Liverpool's European Cup-winning teams. Thompson and one of his team-mates, Sammy Lee, are now integral parts of the Liverpool management team, further cementing the corporate culture Gerard Houllier and the club wishes to both retain and foster. Butt, Scholes, Giggs and the Neville brothers were all brought up in the Manchester area and were mostly keen United fans. Beckham is a Londoner but his family were passionate United supporters.

> A large proportion of the young players whom Shankly and Ferguson introduced were from the local area.

Several football commentators have been of the opinion that Nicky Butt and Philip Neville are not of sufficient ability to be retained within the United squad. But Ferguson has not so far contemplated discarding them. He knows that a strong team spirit has been essential to the club's success in recent years and that this group of players who have grown up together has been largely responsible for its existence. While this group of players remains at the club, players recruited from outside cannot help but be affected by the prevailing ethos and are soon integrated into the United way. As Ferguson said after the capture of van Nistelrooy and Veron:

66 We are very lucky, we seem to transcend that mercenary type of professional you see nowadays, the player who never really settles. It's a good dressing-room, always has been, and both the new players have been quite surprised at the kind of camaraderie we have here. 99

For team spirit to prosper, the manager must impose a transparently meritocratic system. Any perceived lack of fairness or sign of favouritism will cause rifts and poison the atmosphere within the team. Stan Cullis recalled having to tell the great Billy Wright, then 35 years of age, that his playing days were numbered at Wolves:

66 The task of telling Bill I could no longer guarantee him a first-team place was most painful. Yet I should have been failing in my duty at Wolves if I had failed to do that. I have always told my players that the better man always goes into the senior team. If I made an exception, even for Wright, the effect would not have been good on morale and spirit at the club. 99

In previous eras this fairness was also reflected in the pay scales. Roger Hunt, a Liverpool player from the 1960s, says that under Shankly, the players 'all got paid the same as each other with bonuses on top of the basic. It fostered a great team spirit.' Tom Finney suggests that 'Shankly created a happy unit, which was his secret. He thought that it was wrong to have one fellow in the side who was earning twice as much as another because if he's having a bad game, what do the others think?'

This strategy of equal pay might have worked for Shankly in the 1960s, but it is unworkable in the modern business or football world. Stars might be expected to give their all for the team, but they are nonetheless still stars and consequently demand pay commensurate with the quality of their individual contribution to team performance. However, providing the system of pay differentials is transparent it should not endanger team spirit. Alex Ferguson sought for many years to maintain a tight wage structure at United and differentials were kept to a minimum. But in late 1999, in order to retain the influential captain Roy Keane, the club was forced to accede to his financial demands, which reputedly made his salary at least twice that of most of his colleagues. However, his team-mate Gary Neville claimed that the other United players appreciated Keane's value to the team and were perfectly happy to accept that he should be the highest-paid player:

❝We are talking about someone who is the most influential player in Europe and no other player at Old Trafford can have any complaints about what he is being paid. There is no envy from the rest of us. He is the captain and deserves everything he gets. To lose Roy would have been a massive blow. It would not have been a good message for the rest of the players.❞

To maintain team spirit, the manager needs to monitor it constantly and act quickly to remove or discipline negative influences. No player can be bigger than the team. Shankly ensured that no individual was allowed to think of himself as more important than the collective whole. Roger Hunt says that 'anyone who came to Anfield was made aware that it was a down-to-earth place, no superstars'. Shankly stressed that 'all the players got international caps by playing collectively for each other. Every player in my team has to play for the team. Not himself. We do things collectively.'

> Every player in my team has to play for the team. Not himself.

In his autobiography, Ferguson talks of his decision to sell Paul Ince in 1995. Ince had been an important part of the United side which had won the league in the previous two years and was extremely popular with the supporters. However, Ferguson believed that he had become excessively arrogant in the dressing-room, to the point where he was playing according to his own whim, and not for the benefit of the team unit:

> ❝I felt I had to act on my conviction that the fundamental change in Paul's attitude, his insistence on trying to assume a role in the team for which he was not equipped, had diminished his usefulness to us to the point where a transfer made absolute sense.❞

All players must be seen by the other members of the team to be putting in a similar amount of effort and making similar sacrifices. The manager has to intervene if this rule is not observed. The great George Best was indulged by Manchester United manager Frank O'Farrell in the early 1970s when the player continually went missing from his duties at the club for several days at a time to pursue his well-known predilection for alcohol and women. Bobby Charlton believes O'Farrell's failure to clamp down on Best's behaviour had a detrimental impact on team spirit:

❝The spirit was not helped by all the trouble with George Best … three or four times O'Farrell let him off when the players were looking for a lead … If you don't have a club that's happy, you've had it in Division One. If you get this situation, and you come to an important match and ask the players for 100 per cent, they won't give it. Not deliberately, it's just something inside you.❞

Neither does such indulgence help the player. Players such as Best and Paul Gascoigne, another extremely gifted player whose career was blighted by a lack of the requisite discipline off the field, may well have benefited from *not* being treated specially.

In contrast, Ferguson swiftly moved to discipline David Beckham when, citing various excuses, the player missed training on three separate occasions between December 1999 and February 2000. Eventually, Ferguson's patience snapped. He could not let this situation continue when other players worked diligently and conscientiously in training every day, very often to find themselves on the substitutes' bench when the team was selected:

❝It doesn't matter to me how high a player's profile is. If he is in the wrong, he is disciplined. And David was definitely in the wrong. I had to think that David wasn't being fair to his team-mates. Nicky Butt, Phil Neville and Ole Gunnar Solksjaer cannot count on being regulars in our first team, but they are model pros who never miss training.❞

He dropped Beckham very publicly from a crucial game against their nearest challengers, Leeds. The fact that Ferguson chose arguably United's most important fixture to make his stand may have been a coincidence. If so, the effect was perfect. United won without Beckham and Ferguson has had nothing but total commitment from the player since then.

One way for the manager to enhance togetherness within the team is to highlight the existence of an external enemy. The presence of an external enemy, imagined or real, induces the team to forget about any internal disputes and focus on sticking together to fight against those who criticize or threaten them from outside. Ferguson, throughout his managerial career, has employed a siege mentality, a 'them against us' philosophy, to engender team spirit. When he was manager of Aberdeen, he told his players that the whole of the Scottish footballing establishment was willing them to fail. A former player at Aberdeen, Mark McGhee, describes Ferguson's method: 'He gave us a persecution complex about Celtic, Rangers, the Scottish Football Association and the Glasgow media, the whole west of Scotland thing. He reckoned they were all against us: and it worked a treat.'

At United, he has employed similar tactics. He told his players the whole world was against them, the media included. After Jimmy Hill, the then BBC football analyst, criticized an incident of United foul play, Ferguson said:

> **If there's a prat going about in this world, he's the prat. I am not interested in Jimmy Hill ... The BBC are dying for us to lose. Everyone is from Liverpool with a Liverpool supporter's flag. They'll be here every time we lose, that mob – Barry, Bob, Hansen, the lot of them. The Liverpool Supporters' Association.**

The external enemy policy can only be exploited in a business environment where competition (the 'enemy') is highly visible. This might involve a physical market place, such as the former London Stock Exchange or the current London insurance market, where traders or brokers will come across representatives from other companies in their daily routine. Alternatively, the focus on the 'enemy' might also be productive when the team's performance is regularly and formally measured against that of its competition, like in the stock market analysts' league tables which are compiled for various sectors. For most managers, though, the only 'enemies' visible enough to inspire togetherness will be individuals or departments outside of the team but within the same company. This might generate team spirit but will clearly not assist the development of interdependence and exchange of knowledge within the company as a whole.

For the team to function effectively as a unit, there must be a defined and realizable collective goal which each individual within the team genuinely wants to achieve. The goal, like the 'enemy', enables the members of the team to focus on what they have in common, not what sets them apart. In football, a goal might be a trophy, a position in the league (such as Liverpool's pursuit of a Champions League place) or the avoidance of relegation in a particular season. In business, a goal might be an annual target of a certain amount of revenue or the acquisition and retention of a particular account. The goal must be decided by the team itself and be clear and easily measurable. Every member of the team must believe that their own best interests can only be realized through the team.

Lesson

No single player is greater than the team. Only *through* the team can players realize their potential.

The talent economy

IS THERE A TALENT WAR? IN BUSINESS THAT MIGHT BE A LEGITIMATE question, in football it's a nonsense question. Of course there is a talent war. Why else would Real Madrid, an organization hugely in debt, pay £37 million for Luis Figo and then upwards of £50 million for Zinedine Zidane? The only reason is that talent of that calibre is scarce *and* valuable. It is not valuable just because it's scarce, it is valuable because it can make the difference between winning and losing.

In business there has been considerable discussion about the so-called 'war for talent', much of which was generated by an article in *The McKinsey Quarterly* published in 1998 (Chambers *et al.*) and based on the previous year's research on the topic. Companies interviewed by McKinsey reported they were 'chronically talent-short across the board'.

In 2001 (Axelrod *et al.*) the research was updated and found that far from cooling, the talent war was intensifying. Senior managers were reporting that 'A-players – the best 20 per cent or so – raise operational productivity, profit and sales revenue significantly more than average performers'. Not a particularly radical revelation and one that football managers have spent their lives working with.

Every club chairman, for example, will tell you that every manager is always just two players short of the perfect squad and those players are never what Lawrie McMenemy, the former Southampton manager, calls 'the roadsweepers'. They are always what he calls the 'violinists' (the stars). Ron Noades, when both chairman and manager of Brentford, said that whereas all his previous managers, at Crystal Palace and elsewhere, had always wanted additional players, at least as chairman/manager he could avoid that issue. As we left the meeting we asked him if Brentford needed any new players for the next season. 'Just two,' he replied before realizing what he had said and laughing.

In football, and increasingly in business, the difference between winning and losing is heavily dependent on the talent available to be deployed. Just as importantly it is dependent on how that talent is managed and organized. It is the synergy between talent and organization which differentiates the best from the also-rans. Ironically, this point was well made by a professor of organizational behaviour at Stanford Business School who was attempting to prove the futility of chasing talent. In an article published in 2001, Professor Pfeffer argued that 'fighting the war for talent is hazardous to your organization's health'. He reasoned that the 'war for talent' is a distraction from what companies should concentrate on – 'devising systems that get the most out of everyone'.

He makes the same mistake as those who think you just gather up the talent and let it loose. To be successful at the highest level, you need both talent *and* a system. When the talent is not operating at the optimal level, the team should be able to fall back on the system. Chelsea under Gianluca Vialli was a classic example of a lack of consistency brought about by over-reliance on 'talent'. A good rule of thumb for any football chairman should be that if a team is highly successful in cups but fails in the league, then sack the manager. Why? Because the players are only performing

when they feel like it. The manager is not driving the organization, the players are.

Bryan Robson's roller-coaster at Middlesbrough was another high-profile example. Robson was ill served by a well-meaning chairman (Steve Gibson is also a close friend). Had the chairman recognized earlier than he did that while Robson, as a big-name player, could attract stars he could not organize them, he would have insisted that he [the chairman] should have had an input in the selection of the remainder of the management team. Of course, in football, such an idea has traditionally been anathema. Ultimately, however, Gibson was forced to bite the bullet and parachute in Terry Venables as what amounted to a chief operations officer (COO). Naturally, this emasculated Robson, who nevertheless managed to retain a dignity uncommon in the game. Robson proved that the ability to attract talent, which famous ex-players clearly have, is not enough in itself – utilizing that talent is just as important.

> To be successful at the highest level, you need both talent and a system.

Although operational effectiveness will be dealt with in detail in Chapter 9, it is necessary to mention it in this chapter in case the inter-relationship between the two is underestimated. Rather than being hazardous to your organization's health, successfully fighting the talent war can only add value.

What is crucial is ensuring that the talent war is fought to obtain both players and members of the senior management team. Selecting the people whose job it is to get the best out of the staff on an everyday basis is one of the key tasks of senior management and is the one where mistakes are often made. The McKinsey report suggested that 'talent has been the most under-managed corporate asset for the past two decades'. The report also asserts:

> **"**Companies perceived by their employees to be good at managing talent are also the ones doing well in the market ... whether or not these firms really are the best talent managers hardly matters ... if good employees believe that they are working for the best, they will stay put.**"**

Clearly, attracting talent adds little value without the people in place to extract the most value from that talent. The management of talent as a corporate asset is an area where football and business can learn together as they both develop.

When Douglas Daft, chairman and CEO of Coca-Cola, reappointed Brian Dyson as COO in summer of 2001, it was recognition that the best strategy in the world is pointless without those who can execute that strategy. Daft put it very clearly:

> **"**We're on a great path, but my worry is the speed with which we execute. A company like this needs an intense focus in operations and execution. We need to be faster and better. Brian has a great background and is going to give hands-on guidance and accelerate execution.**"**

Daft added: 'I love operations, but can't get into the detail myself.' He would, he said, be concentrating on the company's 'strategic direction'. Daft took the action belatedly as Coke's stock continued to slip while the company failed to reach its growth targets. Dyson was not a young whiz-kid but a 65-year-old proven operations manager. He had 35 years' experience with Coke. The only criterion for selection of managerial talent or,

indeed, any talent must be effectiveness. On 21 June 1999 *Fortune* magazine ran a special edition in which the cover story was, 'Why CEO's fail'. The conclusion was, as mentioned elsewhere, 'bad execution. As simple as that: not getting things done, being indecisive, not delivering on commitments.'

It is clear that the human resourcing problem that modern organizations face is not fundamentally a lack of technically proficient personnel but rather one of a lack of 'skilled' personnel and being managed effectively – being able to make things happen. Here again football provides useful terminology in that it differentiates between 'technique' and 'skill'. Technique is the ability to complete a task – kick a ball from A to B or program some software. Skill is the ability to deliver technique under pressure. Almost every footballer can hit a 1 metre square target from 12 metres. Unless, of course, you apply the pressure of a penalty shoot-out in the World Cup final. Then, even the world footballer of the year, Roberto Baggio, and the man voted AC Milan's all-time greatest player, Franco Baresi, cannot hit an 8ft by 8yd goal. Similarly, the person of value to the corporate team is the one who can deliver his technique under the pressure of time, lack of resources or lack of staff, or indeed any other pressures which may emerge.

Business must begin to define talent in precisely the same way as football – a genius for making things happen, be that completing a project to specification, on time and with the minimum of fuss or inspiring and leading others to do the same. What separates Zinedine Zidane and Luis Figo from Paul Gascoigne or George Best? The minimum of fuss – they are low-maintenance geniuses. They just get the job done.

This is where business and football both have something to learn from their own best practitioners. Only *real* talent is worth fighting for. The best managers can identify the best players in their raw, half-formed or complete versions. And remember, even the best make mistakes. The trick is to cut your losses, a very difficult feat when emotions are involved. The same Alex Ferguson who bought Fabien Barthez, a goalkeeper recognized as one of the best in the world, had previously bought Mark Bosnich and Massimo Taibi, two goalkeepers who turned out to be disappointing recruits for United. What distinguishes Ferguson is an ability to recognize and rectify mistakes.

> The best managers can identify the best players in their raw, half-formed or complete versions.

Ferguson seems partially immune from what psychologists call the 'Concorde fallacy'. The 'Concorde fallacy' is so named because the Anglo-French aircraft was financed even after it became obvious that by any economic calculations it should have been scrapped. This sunk-cost effect is apparent in all organizational spheres. In sport, for example, a 1995 study of the National Basketball Association (NBA) showed that the higher the draft pick, and consequently the higher the cost, the more playing time a player would be given. This enhanced playing time was given irrespective of the player's performance. Similar research in business has generated almost identical results. Data from more than 1,000 firms showed that those businessmen who started their own businesses were statistically much more likely to expand the business than those who bought the business as a going concern. An even more outrageous manifestation of the sunk-cost effect is that the expansions were *more* likely when the businesses began to fail. The ability to be able to recognize and admit mistakes is central to effective management.

THE NEW ECONOMY

The idea that long-term, corporate-wide loyalty is a thing of the past is now current in business. It is a phenomenon with which football managers have long had to live – the recognition that talent will, eventually, walk. What great managers do is ensure that the walkers are the ones they want to walk or are at least willing to allow to walk. It was one of the traits of the great football dynasties that players rarely left them and went on to better things. In his heyday, Brian Clough made an art form out of selling to other clubs players who were never able to reproduce the form they showed under him.

By coincidence, Peter Capelli (2000), a professor of Management Studies at the Wharton School at the University of Pennsylvania, has unwittingly translated the practicality of talent acquisition as always understood by football managers into a theory. He argues that the acquisition and retention of talent is a market-driven process, by which he means a realization that the forces of the market will dictate the movement of talent. He comes up with a particularly useful analogy: 'If managing retention in the past was akin to tending a dam, today it is more like managing a river. The object is not to stop water from flowing but to control its direction and speed.' The best football managers know this intuitively. They seek to hang on to talent for the optimum period. Once a player decides to go, they know it is only a matter of 'when', not 'if'. The art is to either stop him thinking about moving or to make the decision before he does.

What nobody wants, manager or player, in business or sport is a situation where a player is simply serving out his time. When Steve McManaman decided to leave Liverpool at the end of his contract it still had almost a year to run. His performances in his final season were underwhelming. As were those of Sol Campbell

once he had decided to leave Spurs. Liverpool learned the lesson and moved Robbie Fowler on before his sulking presence could further damage the team. Underperforming talent should no longer be considered talent at all.

Talented players can win games – they are the 'earners' not the 'burners' and they directly affect the profit centres. Equally, however, allowing talent to move on too frequently can negatively affect the cost centre. How, for example, do you replace Roy Keane or Patrick Vieira? The answer is, at enormous cost. The cost of the recruitment process, the purchasing fee (including signing-on fee), the wait while the replacement settles into the operational style, if he ever does – all of these factors have to be fed into the calculations before deciding precisely when and how to allow a talent to walk. Development Dimensions International, a human resources consultancy in the US, estimates that the cost of replacing a manager or professional is in the region of $120,000. It is probably a conservative estimate because it estimates training at $15,000. For a newcomer to completely replace an effective worker can take at least six months and probably longer.

It is clear, then, that talent, genuine talent, is worth fighting for and trying to keep. For further proof that football is a good model for the business world, listen to what Bruce Tulgan, author of *Managing Generation X* and *Winning the Talent Wars*, has to say:

66 Rather than the talent wars growing out of a short-term 'hot' economy, there is a fundamental paradigm shift in the employer–employee relationship. From the old, slow-moving, rigid, pay-your-dues-and-climb-the-ladder model to the new, fast-moving, increasingly efficient free market for talent. A free-agent mind-set has swept across the workforce. 99

That speech could have been made by any football employer the day after the 1995 Bosman ruling which allowed footballers freedom of movement in line with EU employment law by preventing clubs demanding a transfer fee for out-of-contract players. In fact, the more astute managers were preparing long before the actual ruling. The difference between football and business is again one of speed. Literally the day after Bosman, agents were proliferating and beginning to circle both clubs and players. Talent as young as eight years old was targeted and signed. The McKinsey report cited earlier (Chambers *et al.*, 1998) noted

> The difference between football and business is again one of speed.

that, in the midst of the war for talent, 'the revenues of search firms have grown twice as fast as GDP [gross domestic product] over the past five years'. Whether it is agents or search firms is irrelevant, those who own talent or can direct employers towards it are making big money – no further proof is necessary to verify the value of talent.

In the best football clubs the talent game is meticulously planned, with well-oiled practices for each aspect of the game. Business would do well not to ignore any element of the talent cycle, shown in Figure 8.1.

As the figure shows, each element of the process overlaps the adjacent element. For example, part of the disposal phase should include searching for replacements and during the retention phase managers must be anticipating disposal. Many companies do parts of the cycle well, but the best do them *all* well. It must be re-emphasized here that the talent we are after are not only the players but also the senior management team.

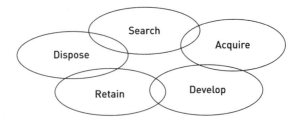

Figure 8.1 Talent cycle

SEARCH

Before analyzing the details of searching for talent, it is worth making reference to the role of brand in the recruiting process. An organization's brand is its first line of recruiting action. A great brand can considerably reduce the search process because it draws talent to the organization like a magnet. For example, every boy would be attracted by Manchester United, but equally parents looking to place their youngsters in football would always be sensible to think of Crewe Alexandra as a first choice. Crewe's manager, Dario Gradi, has created a brand which projects the values of education, integrity, quality coaching and, above all, good sell-on potential. Players can play first-team football for Crewe at an early age and prove themselves to Premier clubs after the normal attrition rate has taken its initial toll.

Leeds United have created a similar brand. Their academy structure, started by Howard Wilkinson, has established a brand that shrieks 'youthful opportunity!' If you're good enough, you are old enough. The brand is reinforced when you pay £18 million for a 22-year-old (Rio Ferdinand) and install him as captain.

The value of branding is, perhaps, an area where football can learn from business where brand is already a powerful recruiting tool. The corporate world puts tremendous efforts into branding. Companies such as Accenture and Booz-Allen & Hamilton, for example, have interactive websites where any visitor to the site is treated like a potential employee and offered advice on the jobs on offer within the company. The same is true of the public sector. The United Nations website, for example, is simultaneously a portal for information and employment opportunities.

If the brand is wrong, the talent will not be drawn naturally to the organization. There needs to be a sympathetic relationship between brand and player. Thus, the first rule of talent searching must be to look for a *good fit* between club and player and the 'fit' must be right in terms of *price*, *culture* and desired *role*.

Price

It's no good coveting Zinedine Zidane if you are in the Second Division. First, you almost certainly wouldn't get him, and second, if you did he would probably ruin the club. When the ageing stars Rodney Marsh, George Best and Bobby Moore went to the then second-division Fulham in the 1970s they injected a quick shot of exhilaration and not much else. For Fulham, at that time, the 'gleesome threesome' probably were the perfect fit. A good time was had by all, but nothing lasting was built. If players are not obviously available at the price you can afford then you need to look further afield. Increasingly in recent years this has meant all corners of Europe.

The business equivalent has been the targeting of the Indian sub-continent for cheap IT expertise. In India, talent is top-class, English speaking, cheap and eager to travel. For those same reasons

South Africa has also been specially targeted. Johann Pretorius, the operations director at the South African company Internet Solutions, says that young, educated whites are being 'snapped up by foreign companies because they speak English, because they are good at what they do and because they are easily persuaded to move abroad'.

In both football and business there are dangers in this process. There have been many failures, such as Igor Stepanovs, who has failed to impress at Arsenal since his transfer from the Latvian club Skonto Riga in 2000, as there have been successes, such as Andrei Kanchelskis, who had an impressive career at Manchester United after he was signed in 1991 from Ukranian club Shakhtyor Donetsk. The prevalence of failures smacks of bad research, bad search procedures, bad agents and bad judgement. The players are not at fault; they look out for themselves but are sometimes simply unable to fit with the requirements of the club. Added to the difficulties of adjusting to a new team culture are the general cultural issues involved with moving to a new country. Although such problems are immediately visible in football, they are just as significant in business. In the US, for example, the downturn in the IT-based economy is leaving many new immigrants from South Asia unemployed and high and dry in a strange land.

Clubs and companies must look beyond the apparent bargain-priced internationals to the precise fit. Can they add value now? Can they be improved? Can they be moved on at a profit? The David O'Leary model provides lessons here. O'Leary said: 'We are trying to buy silver medallists and turn them into gold now. Mark Viduka came for £6 million and how much is he worth now? We don't want to buy people after one last pay-day.'

Eric Thickett, chairman of MiTech Group, a medium-sized, privately owned telecoms company with a phenomenal staff retention record, echoes O'Leary's sentiments and makes a direct footballing analogy. Thickett says: 'We have what we call a "breed Beckham" approach to recruitment. We try to find our own raw talent, both young and old. Just as long as they have the thirst to learn, we train them up.'

Remember, in football as in business, you get what you pay for. If it looks cheap, it's because that's what it's worth at that time. It may be possible to develop the talent, but that takes work and the 'thirst to learn' on the part of the talent. If you want the finished article, you must pay the price.

> Remember, in football as in business, you get what you pay for.

Culture

The price can only be right if the cultural fit is right. As discussed in Chapter 7, it is the responsibility of the manager to create or maintain the team culture. It is his ultimate responsibility, therefore, to select personnel to fit the culture. Both Ruud van Nistelrooy and Juan Sebastian Veron have gone on record as saying that Alex Ferguson's presence at Manchester United was the crucial factor in their decision to join the club. It was Ferguson's personal intervention that swung van Nistelrooy's decision to join United. The player suffered a serious injury when he was originally destined for United and the deal was put on hold. While he was rehabilitating, other clubs came in for him. As van Nistelrooy tells it:

&&I had no obligation to United after what happened a year ago. I also know if I had wanted to put pen to paper, I could be a Real Madrid player right now. But did the Real coach show up at my house when I was grafting and sweating through the rehab? No, he didn't. Only one man came over to see me and that was Alex Ferguson.&&

The culture of intensity, desire, achievement and community established by Ferguson encourages ambitious players to join. Add to that a reputation for being able to handle star players and you have a powerful recruiting tool.

Before searching for a player, recruiters need to be sure that the player will fit the culture. Eric Cantona, for example, was revelatory at Manchester United. However, he was inhibited at Leeds and rejected by France. The best fits are not always the most obvious. Edgar Davids seemed perfect for AC Milan but failed and was revived at Juventus. And who would have thought that European Cup winner Franck Sauzee would find his spiritual home with Hibernian? The only solution to cultural fit during the search process is genuine and high-quality research. Anything less and you are merely storing trouble – ask Harry Redknapp, who surely has the most horrible *mis*-fit stories to tell from his days at West Ham. Marco Boogers, signed in 1995, was sent off in his second appearance for the club, after what was described by *The Sun* as 'a sickening horror tackle'. He then vanished and was discovered some time later hiding in a mobile home in a Dutch caravan park. Florin Raducioiu joined in 1996 and was sold at a loss six months later after apparently missing training for a shopping trip. Portuguese player Dani lasted five months before being thrown out for concentrating too much on nightlife and not enough on football. Javier Margas went missing and was later traced to his home in Chile.

Setting the corporate tone is as essential in business as it is in football. Companies need to match their culture to the place they intend to occupy in the market. Jim Goodnight, founder and CEO of SAS Institute, one of the world's biggest private software companies, developed just such a corporate culture. He recognized that at the height of the dot.com boom he needed to retain talent against the promise of double salary offers. He reasoned that his only competitive advantage would be the company culture. In 2000, *Fortune* magazine placed SAS sixth in its survey of top employers to work for, describing it as 'the closest thing to a workers' utopia in America'.

The company provides free crèches, free doctors on-site, free gym, playing fields, tennis, theatre, canteen and a management which frowns on working any longer than the stipulated 35-hour week. Significantly, this culture is not the result of some altruistic imperative but a calculated bottom-line decision. On-site healthcare, for example, is estimated to save $3 million a year in sick days; a 4 per cent staff turnover rate compared with an industry norm of 20 per cent saves another $50 million in redundancy payments and recruitment fees. The company's policies enabled it to resist other companies' attempts to poach its staff.

Role

If the price is right and the player appears to pass the cultural tests, then only the desired role remains to be satisfied. What do you want this player for? Is he there to provide cover, competition, be 'the man', be the old head, create balance, or provide enthusiasm in the dressing room? Too many managers are seduced merely by availability. They see a great player being pursued by competitors and covet the great man without thinking through clearly what value he will add to *their* team.

When Ferguson talks about the treble, he traces its origins back to three signings made the previous summer: striker Dwight Yorke, central defender Jaap Stam and left-winger Jesper Blomqvist. The least mentioned of the trio is Blomqvist but it was he who enabled the team to continue to function, in balance, when Giggs was unavailable. United later signed another left-sided player, Quinton Fortune, and it is no coincidence that yet another target has been Bixente Lizarazu, another left-sided player who would add further attacking menace on that flank. Ferguson's talent searches are always aimed at providing added value and specific qualities which will enhance the team.

> Too many managers are seduced merely by availability.

Senior management team

Precisely the same principles of talent searching apply to the senior management team. The lesson from football here, however, is a cautionary one. For too long football's recruitment procedure for the managerial team has been the friends and old playing colleagues of the manager. With each new managerial appointment comes an entire new managerial team. Obviously managers must trust their staff, but the concept of professional second-in-command as a sort of an appendage to the boss can be unhealthy for everyone: the boss, the subordinates and the organization. The problem is that in certain instances it has proved hugely successful. Martin O'Neill's team of John Robertson and Steve Walford has gone from strength to strength. If O'Neill had not exercised his power at Celtic to rid the club of any vestiges of the Dalglish/Barnes regime, he may not have been able to alter the culture so rapidly.

Nevertheless, such practices fly in the face of reasonable managerial practice. Adam Crozier, the CEO of the Football Association, argues that the ten managers in nine years of the England team, all with their separate entourages, could only have been detrimental to the England cause. 'Imagine,' he says, 'that at each crisis a company changed its entire management team, how stable would that company's shares be?'

Far better, Crozier believes, that the boss should establish a management layer immediately beneath him, some five or six strong, and all capable of being the boss. It makes little sense, he argues, to seek the best for every post in the organization *except* those close to the top. In football there is a tradition of doing the opposite, of appointing non-threatening friends who act merely as conduits or back-watchers. Important roles, but not sufficient to add maximum value to the organization.

In business, the lesson from football must be that only the best can manage the best. When Brian Kidd left Manchester United, Ferguson did not rush to appoint his successor from within but searched from a very small pool, with very specific criteria, before selecting Steve McLaren. Crozier worked through the same meticulous process to find Keegan's successor after his resignation following the Wembley defeat by Germany. The ultimate choice, Sven Goran Eriksson, is charged not only with creating a successful team on the field but also one off the field. By recruiting the calibre of coaches he has, Eriksson is establishing the equivalent of an elite cadre.

Sir Ian Prosser, the chairman of the brewing giant Bass, created a similar group with his 'chairman's list'. The names on the list can expect accelerated promotion but with it comes increased responsibility. They must adhere to the cultural ethos of the organization, promote best practice and provide a behavioural example of

the company's core values. Of course, only one name on the 'chairman's list', and only one of Eriksson's lieutenants, will be the next boss, but that does not preclude high office for the others who will all have been stretched by the experience of working for, and with, the best. The current crop of French managers working in the Premier league bear testament to the value of an elite cadre policy as employed by the French football association.

Whether the talent being sought is on or off the field, the principles remain the same: look for the right fit – on price, culture and role. Increasingly football will have to upgrade its vaunted but often unsystematic scouting systems. A version of business search agencies (head-hunters) must emerge, not least to deal with the perceived menace of the dreaded agents. Terry Butcher, the former England captain, has, in fact, already established such a search agency. The search for talent is inexorable. The more systematic it can become, the more effective it will be.

ACQUISITION

Having searched for the talent and finally found it, the next stage is to acquire it. How do you convince a player or a member of the senior management team to join you? As stated earlier, the brand is crucial. One agent tells a story, possibly apocryphal, of taking a young player to meet with Manchester United. Prior to meeting the United negotiation team, the agent tells the player: 'Say nothing, let me do the talking, that's what you pay me for.' They walk into the office, sit down. Martin Edwards says to the player: 'How would you like to join us here?' 'Yeah, brilliant,' blurts out the player. The agent rolls his eyes and admits defeat. Such is the power of brand. In cases like this, the brand itself has effectively acquired the talent.

However, if the talent is exceptional, the choice of brands on offer will also be exceptional. Great players gravitate to great clubs. What is it then that makes a player choose between Barcelona, Real Madrid, Manchester United, Milan, Juventus and Arsenal? The answer is, the manner in which the club pursues the player, the way in which the club sells the experience of working for it. Marcello Lippi, who turned round Juventus after some years in the doldrums, says: 'There is only one way to motivate players every time, and that is to appeal to the things they have not yet achieved.' Jerry Wright, the MD of London-based Prism Executive Recruitment, has a similar view of senior executives joining the dot.com revolution. What gets them from the old to the new economy is 'a real buzz. Nothing replaces that excitement, particularly for someone who has experienced the relatively slow pace of the larger corporate environment.'

> Great players gravitate to great clubs.

Juventus look for the raw talent. They took Zidane, for example, from the relatively small Bordeaux club and the majority of their Italian players come from the lower leagues. The attraction, and thus the deal, is simple. Come to Juventus on a relatively modest wage, win championships, catch the eye, become a star – move on. In other words, the experience of working for Juventus will complete your CV.

Only achievement, or the promise of it, can sell the company to the prospective employee. At Leeds, David O'Leary claims that his 'biggest achievement for [the] club is that I have sold the product to players who would not have considered coming here before'. However, the *promise* of achievement will not keep the likes of Harry Kewell, Rio Ferdinand and Mark Viduka very long. Leeds must start to win things, and soon. Towards the end of the 2000/01 season the smell of the excitement of a young team striding to the brink of the Champions League final was fresh in the players' nostrils. By the end of the season they had failed to reach the final and had not qualified for the next Champions League. The next stage will present O'Leary with the ultimate challenge. If Leeds are not to be a dot.com burn-out then O'Leary must keep the momentum going. A great deal of the club's progress has been built on the foundations established by Howard Wilkinson and George Graham, and O'Leary must prove his own credentials because the *promise* of success can be sustained only for a finite length of time. This was a lesson the dot.coms failed to heed.

When players think of winning things they look to associate with winners. Part of the attraction for Gabriel Batistuta, for example, in joining AS Roma in the 2000/01 season, was the presence of Fabio Capello. He had masterminded the Milan dominance of the mid-1990s, moved to Real Madrid for one season and won the Spanish Primera Liga. Batistuta had never won the Italian league (the Scudetto) and Capello was a winner – the attraction was irresistible. Batistuta now has a Scudetto to his name. Time for Capello to move Batistuta on, perhaps.

In business, the challenge for organizations is precisely the same as in football. The challenge is rarely in acquiring talent to a start-up or an exciting project, but in maintaining the momentum such that the attraction for talent remains. This requires an expectation of achievement that is associated with the company or the manager, preferably both. For the company's part, it needs to be acquiring people to take it to the next stage. As clubs enter the Premier League for the first time they will sign a core of players who have been there before. Those players, added to the squad that got them there, will provide a mix the manager believes will enable them to survive.

Similarly, companies entering new fields look to acquire experience. As the public utilities privatize, for example, they look for people who have been through the mill. They look for a deregulation expert, not a gas/utility or water/utility expert. When Virgin Atlantic set up its Revivals lounge, a top-notch lounge 'for upper-class arrivals', it recruited staff from the hotel industry. Going to another industry is one of the few times when it is likely that you will have to break the manager's golden rule – *if you need to advertise, you don't know your business*. Managers who know their business know the talent. Only when you step outside your domain should you need to advertise or hire professional search help. Of course, even going for someone who has been a success in another industry with similar problems is no guarantee of success. The failure of non-railway people at Railtrack is a classic example.

Railtrack eventually forced the incumbent, Steve Marshall, and his chairman, John Robinson, to step aside and appointed an engineer as the new CEO to take them out of receivership. John Armitt, a former chief executive of Costain, the construction and engineering group, brought railway experience plus a strong civil engineering background. He was a former chief executive of Union Railways, the subsidiary responsible for developing the Channel Tunnel Rail Link. His experience was highlighted by Ernst & Young, the administrators running Railtrack, as a key reason for his appointment. It said: 'The railway, its staff and managers need and deserve strong leadership from people who know the railway industry and who combine commercial and engineering expertise.' The appointment appeased those who had complained that the company was being run by accountants.

What is absolutely essential in the acquisition process is to be very clear about the type of person who fits your organization and to be prepared to use any method to get them.

DEVELOPMENT

Once the talent has been spotted and acquired, the next stage is to develop that talent. While such developments are clearly in the interests of the players, that is not the primary reason for thinking hard about development. There is one very pragmatic reason – value added. A developed player will enhance team performance and, in football, will increase his sell-on value. Thus the development costs of Zidane to Juventus can be more than recovered when he moves to Real Madrid for £50 million. Development is also a good reason to encourage players to play for their national teams. Of course, this may not be true for a player from a national side with few other quality players. George Best, for example, did not develop when playing for Northern Ireland.

The management team can also be developed when they are released for international duty. Not only will they develop, they will also have intimate contact with potential 'poachees' for their clubs. In business the equivalent is to encourage attendance at conferences, workshops, seminars and round-tables, but only for strategic reasons. Conferences that are simply 'jollies' must be discouraged, unless they are specifically for 'jolly' reasons, because they do not add to the value of the organization.

However, the advantages of staff development are not as clear in business as they are in football, although they should be. In business, developing talent becomes a strategic choice. Should the company recruit and develop talent or should it hire and fire? The answer from football is clear – do both, as Alex Ferguson does. Build a strong youth development programme (product development), combine it with the purchase of established players with remaining sell-on value (targeted recruitment policy), establish clearly defined core values (corporate ethos) and design a simple but effective game-plan (corporate strategy).

Notwithstanding the value to the club (organization), the player must welcome the development. So, what type of development excites players? There is remarkable consistency between what drives footballers and business people. A report in *The McKinsey Quarterly* entitled, 'How executives grow' (Handfield-Jones, 2000), identified five job experiences that appeal to talented business people. Table 8.1 shows the McKinsey five plus their football equivalents.

> There is remarkable consistency between what drives footballers and business people.

What the experiences identified by McKinsey provide is the sort of super-charged and therefore exhilarating learning environment that no amount of training

Table 8.1 The five job experiences that appeal to talented people

Business	Football
A new job with greater scope	Moving to a new bigger club or a club in a bigger league
Turning a business around	Turning a club around. As a player, like Keegan at Newcastle; as a manager like O'Neill at Celtic
Starting a business	Moving from player to coach or coach to manager
Managing a large project	Becoming an international manager, like Aime Jacquet with his six-year World Cup project
Working abroad	Playing with and against the best – wherever they are

courses can replicate. The McKinsey report cited factors such as increased pressure, working with other equally, and more, talented people, clearly defined responsibility, demanding team work, speedy feedback and coaching as the creators of the type of quality learning environment which attracts talented people.

Development strategies

If it is accepted that development adds value to the organization and the best development includes the elements described in the McKinsey report, then what should organizational development strategies for talented players seek to achieve?

➡ First, players must be stretched. Manchester United's comparative failure in the Champions League since the treble in 1999 has, in part, been attributed to the lack of competition in the Premier League. It is no coincidence, so the argument goes, that in the year of the treble, United were pushed to the limit on all three fronts.

➡ Second, talent must be surrounded by talent. Such an environment increases the stretch but also increases the role models from whom to learn.

➡ Third, the value of learning must be championed in the club. Learning is not a particularly valued trait in the 'laddish' culture of football or, indeed, that of the City. It must become so and the enlightened managers will see to it that it does.

➡ Fourth, companies/teams must seek 'learning-thirsty' talent.

➡ Fifth, talent must be given its head. Alan Hansen once famously said: 'You don't win anything with kids.'Clearly he had forgotten about the Busby Babes, or he must have mislaid the tape of a 17-year-old Pele scoring two goals in the World Cup Final, or a 22-year-old Cassius Clay beating a

more mature Sonny Liston, or a 17-year-old Boris Becker winning Wimbledon. Genuine talent should not be restrained. The trick, of course – and this is the manager's talent – is to be able to recognize genuine talent when it appears.

The original McKinsey report on 'The war for talent' (Chambers *et al.*) put the development issue into perspective. Organizations, said the report, must 'develop talent aggressively'. This means 'putting people in jobs before they're ready'; 'getting a good feedback system in place'; 'understanding who you are likely to lose if you do not develop them'. The mind-set of aggressive talent development is second nature in football. It is the primary responsibility of the coaching staff. Companies must be brave enough to outsource the current HR function, which is essentially a policing and welfare role, and replace it with director of coaching. This would be a board-level appointment whose job would be to develop the company's central competitive advantage – its talent.

RETENTION

If the talent you have managed to find, acquire and are developing is so central to your team, you had better think very hard about how to hang on to it. Arguably, if Arsene Wenger had managed to retain the services of Nicolas Anelka, Emmanuel Petit or Marc Overmars at Arsenal he may have been able to sustain a genuine challenge to Manchester United. Only when looking at players of this type does the importance of 'retain-ability' become so obvious as an acquisition criterion. For the slightly longer-term interests of the club, is it better to focus on players who look capable of doing the job but are not in such high demand? For example, everyone is searching for high-quality left-sided players for the England team when perfectly adequate players such as Chris Powell and Steve Guppy can do a job. Teams will often pursue precisely the type of player who will prove most difficult to retain.

> Teams will often pursue precisely the type of player who will prove most difficult to retain.

In his *Harvard Business Review* article on 'talent' (2000), Peter Capelli of the Wharton School cites two interesting cases of companies which have questioned the need to concentrate solely on thoroughbreds to the exclusion of workhorses. One realized that morale was being damaged by in-fighting and jockeying for position among the elite and switched its recruitment targeting from the Ivy League to more modest schools. Its reward was low turnover, high commitment, loyalty and gratitude. The other company deliberately hires one-third of its electronic component assemblers from high-risk applicants, including ex-drug addicts and convicts. Gratitude for the opportunity again translates into loyalty. Giving a player his first chance or an opportunity to resurrect a career can be a key to retention.

Of course, gratitude is not enough and other factors need to be in place, not least the 'fit' we spoke about earlier. As Andy Esparza, vice president responsible for global recruiting at Dell, explains: 'Hire people who fit what you value.' Should Wenger, therefore, have thought more carefully about how retainable were Anelka, Petit and Overmars before buying them? In reality, could he have done so? In the high-remuneration, high-talent environment of the financial markets, for example, the answer may be no.

It may be that the talent is so rare that compromise on the reten-

tion criteria might be the only answer. Manchester United under Ferguson *have* managed it by promoting a culture of loyalty.

Surveys of opinion in the markets of New York and London, for example, show that close to 50 per cent of city workers expect to spend only another year in their current job and a further 20 per cent plan to move within two years. Only 12 per cent said they would stay in their jobs for more than four years. An Institute of Management survey (Rice, 2000) found that 43 per cent of Britain's senior managers and professionals said their 'loyalty is to their own careers and not to their employers'. In the talent industries only success is valued and once it has been achieved, incentives to stay must be increased. It's catch 22 – if the team is not successful, the talent will look elsewhere; if it is successful, the talent will seek new challenges. It becomes a primary task of the manager to provide such challenges. Managers must appreciate what it is that will appeal to different people.

The easiest to deal with are those with intense inner drive. They select their own challenges. Fabien Barthez chose United because his insatiable appetite for success was matched by Ferguson's. Having settled in to United he admits to being 'surprised by the quality of the Premiership and the warmth of Ferguson'. Not two of the most obvious comments we expected to hear. Nevertheless, he is now settled and can concentrate on his obsession with success. Boudewijn Zenden, by contrast, is quoted as relishing the challenge of *resurrecting* an underachieving team at Chelsea. His midfield partners, Frank Lampard Jnr and Emmanuel Petit, also saw Chelsea as a vehicle for their own challenges. It is doubtful whether any of the three were attracted solely by the manager, but the manager will have carefully used the circumstances to appeal to each of them.

Business managers must do the same. What was it, for example, that persuaded hordes of 30-something high-flyers to desert the big consultancies for the dot.com start-ups? It clearly wasn't salary because generally they were reduced by as much as 75 per cent. It also wasn't security because it was a volatile sector. Whether it was eventual fabulous wealth, the challenge, or simply the buzz, a manager wishing to retain these people had to feed the emotion that had attracted them initially. Managers have to understand what drives individuals. While accepting that challenge is the most important factor, it is nevertheless worthwhile establishing a checklist of other more mundane factors which are likely to influence the retention of talent.

Pay

Probably the least important is pay. Report after report places pay between fifth and seventh on the list of importance in job selection/satisfaction. Sol Campbell chose Arsenal over foreign clubs despite reputedly being offered considerably more money to move abroad. Naturally, if the pay differential is huge, it may increase in significance. Pay must be generally comparable within the sector. Consultants may have dropped from £300,000 to £75,000 to hook-up with a dot.com but they would not have dropped from £100,000 to £10,000. However, if it's their own company and the money is burning fast, they may even forgo a wage in order to hang in there. Pay is rarely the main driver.

Perks

Neither are perks, although they are becoming more significant than pay as they become more creative. The type of accommodation, transport and clothing a member of staff can expect as he moves from organization to organization are carefully considered. Particularly with young, emerging talent, the accoutrements of success are important life-style considerations. Supplying your greatest prospects with BMWs or Mercedes or membership of an elite leisure club may be the perk that convinces them to come and/or stay. Or, as in the case of SAS cited earlier in this chapter, the whole culture of the company acts as a massive perk.

Location

For some, location can be the single most important factor. Did Sol Campbell simply want to stay at home? Location is going to be increasingly significant as global movement of labour increases. London clubs will eventually dominate as the location of choice for star foreign players in Britain. Unlike many countries, Britain has only one world-class city: London. Manchester, Birmingham and Liverpool are second-tier. Transport into and out of London from abroad is easier, entertainment is more diverse and anonymity is easier to achieve. In football terms, London will become what Rome, Milan, Madrid and Barcelona are in their respective countries.

> The idea that talent is attracted to rural outposts because of quality of life is nonsense.

In business, cluster locations will also continue to dominate, despite the ability to work virtually. Financiers will gravitate to London, New York, Tokyo, Shanghai and Frankfurt; 'techies' will go to Silicon Valley or MS city. The idea that talent is attracted to rural outposts because of quality of life is nonsense. Talent goes where the action is. Action for the talented is career related. If

Manchester United are ever toppled from the elite group, they will find it hard to attract and retain talent. Currently their brand, their success and Alex Ferguson are magnets. Location has always been an important retention criterion and will continue to be so.

Transition

Similarly, the transition period is a vital ingredient in the retention process. How players settle in, and how long it takes, can either reinforce or undermine retention. The refrain of players 'unable to settle' has become all too common. It was bad enough when players moved between regions of the country, but now that movement is global the difficulty is exacerbated. Extensive research into the background and personality of the players is essential in managing this issue. The use of psychometric profiling, such as that pioneered by Jacques Crevoisier with the French national team, and presumably imported by him to Liverpool when he was appointed by the club in May 2001 as first-team coach, is aimed primarily at predicting performance levels. More needs to be done on personality traits aimed at assisting with the transition phase. Research at the Cranfield School of Management shows 'that for 55 per cent of the executive population the learning curve averages out at about 30 months'. Clearly, easing transition for incoming staff is good value for any effort expended.

What good management requires is that talented joiners are integrated into the organization as quickly as possible and that includes the various cultural aspects of the new environment. These would be both internal and external cultures. The primacy of the needs of the team ensures that new players are immediately embraced into the internal organizational culture by the management in order to extract maximum value as quickly as possible. External cultural factors are more difficult to accommodate, especially when players are now moving between continents with all the attendant language difficulties. This is where organizations in large cosmopolitan locations have a clear advantage. The French contingent at Arsenal and the Italians at Chelsea, for example, often comment on the ease with which they can either fit in with big city culture or find other French and Italian groups with whom they can mix.

Although management may do everything possible to accommodate incoming players, there is another side of the coin – the resistance of incumbent players. Is the new player going to replace me? Is he going to replace my friend? Generally the two imperatives tend to balance each other in football. In best practice they combine. Anyone witnessing the genuine pleasure for van Nistelrooy on the faces on his new colleagues when he scored his opening goals for Manchester United would have seen the results of a well-oiled integration machine. Ferguson has created an environment where talent is recognized and welcomed. It is not viewed as a threat but as something which adds competitive advantage to the team. Only the team counts. That is Ferguson's secret – it's that simple and that difficult.

Ferguson does not have to deal with one of the problems that afflict business. Businesses feel the need to expand. As they do, the workforce increases and managers begin to lose touch and as a consequence the 'team-ness' somehow dissipates. Even the close relationships in companies such as Virgin Atlantic, which start out as very close-knit operations, are stretched as the company expands. The ethos and culture that propelled them in their battles against the giants are gradually lost as the number of employees increases and contact becomes more difficult. Football

teams are protected against this phenomenon and it is interesting to reflect how well Ferguson might do as the CEO of a huge organization.

Many companies are attempting to combat the phenomenon by the introduction of mentoring systems. Yet this practice cannot replace contact with the ultimate decision maker. Irrespective as to how valued the coach tells you that you are, you need to know the manager's thoughts – he picks the team. The McKinsey report (Chambers *et al.*, 1998) states that:

66 Two very well-run companies recently discovered that several high performers had no idea that they were highly regarded and were being groomed. 99

They needed to hear it from 'the man' himself.

The thorny problem of ethnic clusters is another transitional issue. It may be easier to assimilate groups of French players or Dutch players than to welcome individuals but such a practice risks diluting the perceived traditional British strengths. This has been a cause for concern at Arsenal. Thierry Henry understands British concerns and astutely observes:

66 You have to move with the world. Everyone is moving – everyone is playing everywhere. I know it isn't easy to accept because when you live on an island you are always more protective of your island – it's the same for me in the West Indies ... I can understand this point of view but as I said, you have to move the way the world is moving. 99

Henry explains that great efforts are made to avoid any Franco-ization at the club and they are mostly successful. As with

Arsenal, the Italian and French dominance at Chelsea has been cited as a difficulty and the Dutch takeover under Louis van Gaal at Barcelona caused enormous tensions.

In business, the large influx of national/ethnic groups with specific talents or lower salary expectations causes the same problems. The tensions with the indigenous group can disrupt the company. This is true even if, as is now more common, the work is outsourced. The outsourcing of IT work to the Indian sub-continent raises the same protectionist hackles as does the influx of foreign players. It must be recognized, however, that as globalization of labour increases, the situation will need to be managed, not resisted.

> The tensions with the indigenous group can disrupt the company.

The job

Once a player is in the club and the transition period navigated, what is it that keeps him there? One factor is the precise nature of the job itself. Along with brand, McKinsey regards this as joint top factor in what motivates talent. When Johan Cruyff banished Gary Lineker to the flank position at Barcelona, the writing was on the wall. When Petit was forced by van Gaal, also at Barcelona, to play in central defence or when Ruud Gullit was forced wide by Arrigo Sacchi at AC Milan, it was clear that the situation could not continue. Players have favourite positions (jobs) and one way to retain them is to design roles for which they are best suited and for which they feel best suited.

Psychologists Timothy Butler and James Waldroop put it very clearly (1999):

> **❝** In these days of talent wars, the best way to keep your stars is to know them better than they know themselves – and then use that information to customize the careers of their dreams. **❞**

They revealed that their research, conducted over 12 years, suggests that 'many talented professionals leave their organizations because senior managers don't understand the psychology of work satisfaction; they assume that people who excel at their jobs are necessarily happy in their jobs'.

The flip side of this argument is that the individual's interests must not be accommodated to the detriment of the team. David Beckham may well prefer centre-midfield, but his value to the team on the flank cannot be replicated by any player in the world – in the middle United have Keane, Butt, Scholes and Veron. Similarly, Marcel Desailly's desire to play at centre-back was accommodated by Milan only if it was in the team's interest. Mostly he operated, with the young Demetrio Albertini, in centre-midfield. The manager's task is to balance the wellbeing of both the team and the individual.

Status

Sometimes it is not only the precise playing role that exercises the mind of players but also their status within the team. Leadership on the field is a quality much valued by managers. Walter Smith, the former

Everton manager, says it's something you can spot immediately. 'Not necessarily the best player,' he says, 'but the leader; an essential ingredient in any successful team.' Whether that leader is a thoughtful Danny Blanchflower, a swash-buckling Dave Mackay, a manically possessed Graeme Souness, an imperturbable Bobby Moore or an imperious Franz Beckenbauer, every team needs a focal point in the hierarchy; and everyone needs to know their place in that hierarchy.

While the drive for team-ness is at its most obvious in football, it is also commonly recognized that hierarchical structures within the team are inevitable. The informal rules of dressing-room hierarchy must be understood by any successful manager. Equally his distance from that dressing-room must be maintained. The dressing-room is a special place and managers transgress the unwritten rules at their peril. The number two acts as a buffer and a conduit between the dressing-room hierarchy and the manager and as such plays a vital role (see Chapter 6). The intuitive ability of football managers to deal with the complexity of such hierarchical structures provides a powerful model for business.

Also, despite the overt drive for flatter, less hierarchical organizational structures in the corporate world, status-hunger is alive and well. A 2000 study conducted at the INSEAD business school by Christoph Loch reasserted the importance of status signals in the attraction and retention of staff. He argues that the flat-structure advocates are fighting against genetic pre-programming. It has been shown that the chemical 'serotonin', which encourages feelings of wellbeing, actually rises when staff are promoted.

Professor Adrian Furnham, a psychologist at University College London, has stated that 'the desire for status is a powerful force – companies should not try to suppress it'. He even asserts that

'people are willing to trade down salary if it means trading up status'. This is clearly true and it can be damaging. For example, the first attempt (1999) by Glaxo Wellcome and SmithKline Beecham to merge floundered on the alpha male egos of Sir Richard Sykes and Jan Leschly.

However, the motivational aspect of status is not true of everyone. Status does not motivate us all. The most sensible advice to managers must be: 'Know your people, understand their needs, satisfy those needs within the parameters of what adds value to the team.' It is the balance between satisfying the needs of the individual and those of the team which the best managers strike so well.

In business, the remoteness of many CEOs, which tends to increase as their tenure lengthens, means a lack of knowledge of their people, with the consequent turnover problems. In football this rarely happens. Even the most notorious of absentee managers, like Brian Clough, knew their staff intimately. They were so involved in the acquisition process that the players also knew them. Of course sometimes, as with Gary McAllister, for example, Clough's abrasiveness frightened off potential acquisitions (see Chapter 9). That is a good thing. It saves both parties time, money and pain.

DISPOSAL

Clearly, such transparency does not always avoid mistakes. The unfortunate Justin Fashanu, for example, signed as one of the first million-pound players in 1981, was totally unsuited to a Clough regime. Having made such a mistake, how should Clough have handled the situation? Not by banishment and ostracization. But how? The final element of the talent cycle is disposal. How do you get rid of talented players?

The research carried out by McKinsey on this (Chambers *et al.*, 1998) shows that 'taking action to deal with poor performers is the most difficult, least-exploited talent-building lever for any company'. A team with known weak performers, who continue to stay employed, does not attract high performers. The answer to the question of how best to dispose of staff is simple – with the least damage to your team. The first rule for disposal is for *you* to make the decision. Anticipate decline in performance, anticipate a desire to move, anticipate disgruntled team-mates – *anticipate*. Anticipation requires excellent intelligence. This is where the number two adds the most value to the organization. His primary task is to be the manager's antennae in the dressing-room, to gather intelligence on the players. He can say whether disposal is necessary.

> The first rule for disposal is for *you* to make the decision.

Sometimes a change of role is all that is needed and a player can remain with the team. When performance in one role is beginning to deteriorate, consider moving a player to a different role. Ray Kennedy, for example, was less than impressive for Liverpool in the attacking role he had previously occupied for Arsenal. When he was moved to left-midfield he gained a new lease of life. Similarly with Gareth Southgate, from mid-field to central defence; the list is endless. What the players on any such list will have in common is dependability. Form may suffer, but character does not disappear. If, in your company, you have someone with the right character, work hard to get them in the right job before you release them. You may think you are getting rid of an inadequate attacker whereas you have actually released a great mid-fielder.

The same principles are true for movements in status. Downgrading someone is always difficult but it can be done. The rota-

tion systems in football have made this more common. Creating an atmosphere where players of the calibre of Ole Gunnar Solksjaer are prepared to be bit-part players is extremely difficult. The way in which Shane Warne accepted his reassigment from main strike bowler to a support role with the Australian cricket team is an object lesson. His behaviour has been an example of great team behaviour.

The alternative to intelligence-based anticipation is to plan redundancy. The process by which Marcello Lippi moved on his key players during his successful period at Juventus meant that decline in form was never an issue. Players were moved on at their peak and replaced by others with potential. This guaranteed motivation and kept the bank balance healthier. Players like Christian Vieiri, Gianluca Vialli and Fabrizio Ravanelli, all European Cup winners, realized huge profits for the club. Certain Wall Street investment firms have used much the same employment strategy. They require junior analysts to leave after three years. They then know who will leave and when. They can plan succession and design projects around analysts' tenure. The analysts can also plan and can use success in the projects for leverage in their negotiations for their next job.

Having made the decision that someone is leaving, for whatever reason, what are the other rules of disposal?

→ Have at least two replacements in the pipeline, one of equal standing and one with potential. Price will be of importance in which player is chosen.

→ Carefully manage the outgoing player. During his run-down period, he must continue to make a contribution. Be sure they don't hurt you while they're waiting to go. As the HR director of Arrow Electronics said: 'After we have made the decision to remove someone from a job, [we treat] the person with velvet gloves to make the transition as easy as possible.' If it is not possible to manage them, then move them on quickly.

➡ Carefully manage the remaining players. Reassure them that

this is not a trend, that the team will actually benefit.

➡ Make sure they don't go anywhere they can hurt you. In football, the folk-lore of ex-players returning to score the winning goal against their old clubs is well established.

The value of talent has always been obvious in football, both with management and with the players. Combine talent with hard work and organization and you have a winning team. In business there have been counter-arguments to this view that seek to undermine the primacy of talent, especially leadership talent, and promote systemic factors as the key indicator of corporate success. Football people understand the importance of talent because it is the key differentiator on their bottom line – results. All other things being equal, the team with the best players will win. Those who advocate a systemic approach are partially correct. Organizations should have a finely tuned system, which targets, acquires, develops, retains and disposes of talent for the greatest advantage of the team. To do that they must understand what motivates talented employees. If they can isolate those factors and appeal to them, the talent war can be won.

Phil Harkins, the CEO of Linkage Inc., a leading provider of organizational development and corporate education programmes, says quite clearly:

66Companies must find a way to know who their best are, figure out what those employees want and need, make sure that they are getting it, and make sure they know that they're getting it. The old rules of treating everyone the same are for the Old Economy.99

If organizations continue to approach the talent cycle in a haphazard and unsystematic manner, they may get lucky on occasion but ultimately they will lose. In an interview with *FT Dynamo*, Bruce Tulgan made the point precisely:

66The talented people who can't negotiate the best deals for themselves are going to get left behind. And employers that can't negotiate with the best talent won't be able to keep people around long enough to get all the work done. Welcome to the real new economy.99

The real new economy is, of course, the talent economy.

Although in this chapter we have concentrated on the role of talent in the success of teams, it must not be forgotten that the

star players cannot operate without the workers, and that those workers make up the majority of any team. John Knell, author of a recent Industrial Society report, explains: 'The war for talent doesn't go very deep at all. It only impacts about 10 per cent of the workforce, an elite segment of the workforce.' Companies cannot, therefore, simply rely on star performers, as Chelsea have

Lesson

There is a new economy based around the acquisition and retention of talent. Make sure you attend to every aspect of the 'talent cycle'.

found out to their cost in recent years. Before paying excessive sums, football clubs and businesses must ask the question: what produces the results? The answer is the integration of talent into a hard-working and well-structured organization.

Operations

Eventually, after all the planning, strategic analysis and recruitment, the players have actually to play. Soldiers have to fight battles, workforces have to complete projects. In football the general manager is simultaneously the operations manager and as such highly valued for that skill. In business the operations director can often be less valued than the finance director and the marketing director. Clearly those responsible for the operational activity which actually generates the product should be as highly valued as any other member of the team. This chapter looks at those aspects of everyday management that directly affect the result of the battle, the project or the match. We look at the manager as operations director.

The greatest football managers have rarely been *most* respected for their tactical prowess. Peter Shilton says that under Brian Clough, 'tactics never really came into it ... Everybody knew their jobs and we basically let the opposition worry about us ... But we never went into anything elaborate.' When Frank Clark was asked what coaching sessions were utilized to get the Forest back four as slick as they were, he explained that there were none. 'Cloughie just left it to us to work it out.' Tom Saunders recalls that Bill Shankly's chosen playing methods for his team were also very straightforward:

“Many people came here to watch training sessions in those years thinking there was some kind of particular magic and they'd come down to Melwood ... and they'd feel cheated. They would say, 'Well, you mustn't be showing us it all. You must be hiding something from us.' The whole method was simple. It was based on a rapport with management, good management, good players and the freedom to express themselves.**”**

Alex Ferguson believes that the actual effect of tactics, while significant, is frequently overestimated: 'When critics of our game parade their theories about the attributes that lift certain teams above others, I am always amused by their eagerness to concentrate almost exclusively on technical and tactical comparisons. Frequently they discuss football in abstract terms, overlooking the reality that it is played by creatures of flesh and blood and feeling. Tactics are important, but they don't win football matches. Men win football matches.'

What great football managers do share, according to the testimony of those who played under their management, is the capacity to motivate individuals. John Adair, the management expert in the concept of leadership in business, defines motivation as 'getting people to do willingly and well those things which have to be done'. We have seen in Chapter 7 how football managers have sought to generate team spirit in order to maximize collective performance. But what techniques have they used to motivate their players on an individual level?

COMMUNICATION

For people to be able to execute a task, they must first understand exactly what the task is. Clear communication of instructions is, therefore, essential. Even complex ideas need to be conveyed in unambiguous language. Keith Burkinshaw, a former Tottenham manager who played at Liverpool in the Shankly era, describes Bob Paisley's ability to get his point across:

> Even complex ideas need to be conveyed in unambiguous language.

> 66 There was absolutely nothing fancy about Bob. He just got right to the meat of the problem immediately. There were no fancy words with him and he stripped everything to the bone. The players knew this and they responded and reacted to the plain way he said things. 99

Gerry Taggart, the Leicester City player, says that Martin O'Neill 'analyzes things and knows what he wants, but then puts it across simply, with passion, so you know exactly what is expected'.

One reason for the perceived dearth of English management talent both in football and in business might be precisely the manner in which English managers tend to over-elaborate when trying to communicate. The early success of the England manager, Sven Goran Eriksson, led to calls from the Confederation of British Industry (CBI) and Institute of Directors to emulate his ostensibly intelligent approach to management. Julian Birkinshaw, a lecturer at London Business School and an expert in the much-vaunted Swedish management style, believes that the Swedes exhibit 'a curious mix of politeness and straightforwardness, unlike the British system of talking around issues' (*The Times*, 5 September 2001).

However, Eriksson's success may have less to do with a peculiarly Swedish management style and more to do with his personal style and also the fact that he is foreign. Eriksson possesses what

Jim Collins, in his book *Good to Great*, calls 'quiet leadership'. There are plenty of Swedish managers who can compete with the volatile Ferguson. Equally, Ferguson has been just as successful with his style as Eriksson has with his. The advantage that being foreign has is simply not being one of us. Foreign managers are different. When Marks and Spencer chooses a Belgian, the Dome chooses a Frenchman or Ford chooses an Australian, they buy the advantage of difference and the honeymoon period that provides. The problem for the chosen man, however, is that when things go wrong that difference becomes a stick with which the shareholders and the media can beat the organization.

CONFIDENCE

Notwithstanding the importance of the problems of communication identified by Julian Birkinshaw, it is even more important for a manager to ensure the commitment of individuals to completing the tasks he has actually communicated need to be done. The best football managers have first and foremost sought to achieve this by making their players feel valued, praising their individual successes and by promoting an aura of self-belief. Alex Ferguson was asked in an interview which phrase he used most. His response, 'Well done', explains much about his management style. John Murphy, a scout at Aberdeen when Ferguson was manager, says of him: 'I know of nobody who is better at getting the best out of his players than him. He could do it with the kids, the older players and his staff. Everyone. You always did your best for him because he believed in you.'

Robin Taylor, who played for Huddersfield when Shankly was manager, says that he himself was 'never a brilliant player, but he (Shankly) always made you feel an important part of the club'. Brian Hall, a Liverpool player under Shankly, explains that 'the whole philosophy was simple, you were the best and you never questioned it. The self-belief and confidence were endemic.' John Robertson's comments in turn demonstrate how much a person's self-confidence and belief can be increased by the merest show of appreciation from a manager:

‟When I played for Brian Clough, I just wanted to get a 'well done' from him. When I was playing, if ever I did anything right, he always used to get his little hand up and call me and when that happened, I used to feel ten feet tall.”

David Platt recounts how Graham Taylor's team talks at Aston Villa and England gave him the confidence to excel:

‟Each individual got three or four minutes as part of a rhetoric. I'd walk out of the place thinking there wasn't a player that could touch me. I remember we played Man United and even with the likes of Bryan Robson, he'd just end his rhetoric by saying, 'I'd back your engine against his.'”

He adds:

‟Not only did I have full confidence in my own abilities, I also used to have full confidence in my team-mates because he'd built them up so much.”

Youngsters who have not had the chance to experience the personal achievement and success conducive to self-belief are particularly in need of encouragement and praise. Eric Harrison believes that a major element of his role as manager of the

Manchester United youth team was to build up the confidence of his charges:

> **If I've had an influence – and I hope I have – it's a mental one. I used to sit young players down and have one-to-ones with them … It's taken hours and hours, but probably the biggest impact I've had is by telling them individually how good they are. If I thought they were going to play in the first team, I'd tell them so.**

Alex Ferguson himself set the tone of taking time out to encourage young players early in their career. Wes Brown recalls:

> **My first memory of him is coming off the pitch after an under-14 game. He gave me a pat on the shoulder and said, 'Well played lad. Stick at it and you'll do well.' That meant an awful lot to a kid of 13 but it was typical of the boss. He went to loads of junior games to offer encouragement and make the boys feel special.**

SITTING OUT

Some people within any team might not be selected from time to time to participate in a particular project or task and might therefore feel excluded and possibly disillusioned as a result. Such people need special attention from the manager to ensure their continued motivation. This is something which the modern high-level football manager, in charge of sizeable squads who cannot possibly all play in every game, has constantly to bear in mind. As Sven Goran Eriksson says: 'In today's football, with 60 matches per year, you really need two complete teams. So the regular players also have to sit on the bench now and then ... It's important to encourage players in this situation and talk to them more than usual.'

This is a phenomenon increasingly important in business. Much has been made of the 'Hollywood-ization' of modern business project management. This refers to the bringing together of disparate groups to form a short- to medium-term project-specific team. As these teams take centre stage in often glamorous projects, others are required to remain in unsung support positions. As much time must be given to the supporting players (the substitutes) if long-term objectives are to be fulfilled. It is easy to neglect the support players and to be surprised when their commitment is less than total when they are called upon.

> It is easy to neglect the support players and to be surprised when their commitment is less than total.

In business, of course, 'support' is often a permanent position. So too with the off-the-field back-up teams in football, which is why the managers who take time with everyone are always well liked and respected throughout the club. They cultivate that respect. Those responsible for the kit, the ground, the catering, the training facilities, etc. are always given special moments by the best managers. Clough's legendary rapport with the support staff in his clubs, even to the police who manned the ground on match days, was a source of strength in a small club. His insistence that the players did the same was also crucial.

Bobby Charlton recalls how Matt Busby was a master at involving everybody in the club:

66The youngest apprentice, the washer woman, the chap who sweeps out the stand – he knew them all by their Christian names. It may not sound a lot, but it is amazing how good it makes you feel. It emphasizes that you are just as much part of the club as any of the first-team players, that you are part of the Manchester United family.99

CRITICISM

Occasionally it is necessary for a manager to criticize an individual member of his team. Managers take different approaches to this thorny issue. Most managers, on most occasions, prefer to criticize in private and not in front of others. Brian Hall recalls that 'Shanks would have his press conference outside the dressing-room after the game and the press boys could hear what was said before he went out to see them. He'd come in and blast us and the press lads would take that as a cue. "Brian Hall didn't play too well today, Bill." "Great, what a player, what a performance." So we knew damn well that he'd defend us in public.' George Aitken, who played for Workington Town under Shankly, says that 'he would never humiliate you in front of the others, he'd pull you aside if he wanted to have a go at you'.

In 1995, Eric Cantona created international headlines by jumping into the crowd to assault a spectator. Whatever Alex Ferguson said to Cantona in private, he never once criticized him in public for this incident. Shortly afterwards, Ferguson said: 'Eric knows he can depend on me. He knows I don't desert my players. They get it between the eyeballs generally if it's a criticism, but Eric knows that whatever happens it will be in the dressing-room or in my office and that's the end of it.' When David Beckham went to the World Cup with England in 1998, he was omitted from the team to start the first game. Glenn Hoddle, the then England manager, subsequently arranged for Beckham to undertake a press conference. Ferguson, angry that his player should be subjected to such public humiliation, criticized Hoddle in a newspaper article, and later wrote in his autobiography:

> Obliging an emotionally devastated 23-year-old to face a mass interview, during which he was expected to go over the details of his disappointment, reopening the wounds ... struck me as an example of bad human relations.

Defending players in such a way helps to develop a strong bond between the manager and individual players. Steve Bruce, the former United captain, said Ferguson 'protects his players to the hilt ... and we all respect him for it'. Not criticizing his players in front of outsiders is an explicit man-management technique of Ferguson's: 'My job is not to criticize my players publicly. When a manager makes a public criticism, he's affecting the emotional stability of a player and that cannot be the professional thing to do.' However, this is not a one-way understanding and it is not an understanding made for the benefit of the players. For Ferguson his protection is part of a bargain. As he says himself: 'I will always steadfastly defend my players. I will do anything for my players, but in exchange I expect a lot.'

Tom Cannon, of the Kingston Business School, supports the idea that the twin strategy of both public and private praise and support but only private criticism is an essential feature of good management:

> Praise reinforces other aspects of behaviour that link with high levels of motivation and outstanding performance. Building a feeling

of self-worth and a sense of progress are especially important in stimulating outstanding performance. Emphasis on the positive does not eliminate the need for criticism or reform. It means that the most effective criticism is carefully directed with clear messages about how to overcome the problem.**

He reiterates:

The least effective criticism is public, because it quickly translates into blame and forces those attacked to defend their position.

The potentially negative consequences of criticizing players in front of others can be illustrated by an example involving Ferguson himself. While he might never criticize players in front of outsiders, the passion generated by a match atmosphere caused him on one occasion to launch into a tirade against his then goalkeeper, Peter Schmeichel, in front of other team members, after United let slip a three-goal lead against Liverpool in 1994. Schmeichel takes up the story:

I didn't think that was fair. We ended up having a massive, massive row. The more we said to each other, the worse it got. Obviously I stepped over the line. The next day he was in the office. I was called in and he said, 'Listen, I have to sack you. I can't tolerate my players speaking to me like that. It goes against my authority.'

Ferguson was able to back down without losing face when Schmeichel apologized to his team-mates. Had Schmeichel not done so, Ferguson's outburst in front of the team would have deprived him of his great goalkeeper and would probably have cost him as a consequence many of the trophies United were to go on to win in the coming years. It is important for team morale that outsiders as well as insiders understand that nobody is above the team. As in most things, the judgement about managerial criticism is delicate and intuitive.

THE PSYCHOLOGICAL CONTRACT

Shortly after the 33-year-old Don Revie took over as Leeds manager in 1961, he asked Matt Busby for some advice on how to go about his task. Busby replied: 'All you have to do is treat your players well, be honest with them and never lie to them. In return, they'll do anything for you.' This is the essence of a type of psychological contract between management and players which top football managers have sought to implement. Mark McGhee, formerly of Aberdeen, says of Alex Ferguson: 'He put pressure on you to perform all the time and he expected you to have the mental strength to withstand it. If you repaid him, he was incredibly loyal to you … But if you didn't, he wasn't slow to tell you.' Ferguson's thinking here was to institute a completely open and transparent two-way process, based on an unspoken but clear understanding. Ferguson supports the player if he displays the necessary commitment. If the player balks from this commitment, he will do so knowing the potential consequences.

> All you have to do is treat your players well, be honest with them and never lie to them.

The manager must also keep his side of the bargain to ensure the continued loyalty and commitment of his team. As Busby said, the manager must be honest and fair with his players and keep any promises he makes. An example involving Stan Cullis in the 1950s highlights this issue very well. Cullis had introduced a benefit system whereby every player who had served for five years was awarded £750 by the club. Cullis ensured that the benefit was awarded even if the player was a reserve with few first-team appearances. For instance, the player Malcolm Clews was handed the benefit even though he had played just one match in the first team. Cullis had fulfilled his side of the bargain to the letter. Not giving Clews the money might potentially have reduced the force of the psychological contract, and hence the commitment of the players.

INDIVIDUALISM

The history of football is littered with stories of hugely talented but wayward players who have not realized their full potential. The question of how to deal with very able people who do not conform to a corporate type is a challenge for any manager, in whatever industry. Bill Walsh, the American football coach, believes that sports management is making progress in this regard:

66In the old days, the approach was rather crude. The organization would simply discard a player who did not fit a specific predefined mould. If a player did not conform to the way management wanted him to behave or if he made the organization uncomfortable, it got rid of him. That was the typical response.99

Things are different now:

&&Today, in sports, as elsewhere, individualism is the general rule. Some of the most talented people are the ones who are the most independent. That has required from management a fundamental change in the art and skill of communication and in organizational development. Most important, there has been more recognition and acknowledgement of the uniqueness of each individual.&&

Alex Ferguson's handling of Eric Cantona was a lesson in the management of the talented individualist. First, the timing of his recruitment was such that the arrival of a player like Cantona could be greeted with enthusiasm by other team members (see Chapter 7). Then, instead of attempting to make him conform to be just an ordinary team member, Ferguson showered Cantona with praise (he referred to him constantly as 'mon genius'), defended him robustly in the face of public criticism, and made him the captain and fulcrum of a great United team. If he was going to sulk when he was left out of the team or put on the substitutes' bench, Ferguson had a solution – select him for the team for every game. If he was the most talented player, why leave him out?

From the moment he first met him to negotiate a transfer from Leeds, Ferguson told Cantona how much he valued him: 'I made sure he understood perfectly how much I wanted him and how highly I rated him. That counted for a lot with Eric. He wants to be wanted.' Cantona repaid Ferguson's faith in him with loyalty, commitment and great professionalism. Again the psychological contract had been fulfilled. Ferguson readily accepted that the contract would be tilted more in the player's favour and that his own responsibilities would include more frequent and gushing praise than usual. Whereas the Leeds manager Howard Wilkinson had believed the onus was on Cantona to impress him and to earn his praise, Ferguson was happy to tell Cantona how great he was before he had even kicked a ball for United.

Just as important as the way he treated Cantona was the way he explained that treatment to the others. To a certain extent that psychological contract is as significant as the one with the individual. In Cantona's case it was relatively easy. Cantona's complete professionalism meant that only his style of play had to be accommodated. Other wayward stars of the past such as George Best, Stan Bowles and Alan Hudson flouted all aspects of team discipline. By contrast Cantona was a footballing role model. What Cantona demonstrated was that *for* the team any amount of individualism will be tolerated; *against* the team, none will be tolerated.

THE WHOLE PERSON

Several football managers have gone out of their way to take an interest in the background and personal development of their players and in their life outside the club. Although stopping short of friendship in order to preserve a necessary distance, this policy elevates the relationship above the merely professional and creates a human bond, which can serve to increase employee loyalty when it is tested by short-term professional disappointment or an enticing job offer from a competitor. Don Revie was known for building up a strong relationship with all his players and their wives and families. Cards and presents were given to players' relatives to increase that personal tie between player and club. Bob Paisley sent Liverpool players telegrams wishing them good luck before they were to appear in international matches.

Matt Busby was another who never neglected the human side of his relationships with any employee:

❝I wanted to manage the team as I felt players wanted to be managed. To begin with, I wanted a more humane approach than there was when I was playing. Sometimes lads were just left on their own ... There never seemed to be enough interest taken in players ... From the start I tried to make the smallest member think that he was part of the club.❞

He interacted on a personal level not just with players but, as discussed earlier, with everyone who worked at the club.

CLUB IDENTITY

One final point about managing players is sensitivity regarding the identity of the club, the specific cultural environment in which the manager is working. In 1974, between his successful periods at Derby County and Nottingham Forest, Brian Clough was appointed manager of Leeds United, a team which had been successfully managed for many years by Don Revie. At Derby and Nottingham, Clough's forte was to turn average players into very good ones. These players, whether they liked him or not as a person, always had a deep respect for his abilities as a manager and were grateful for the opportunity he had given them. It is well known that many of Clough's players did *not* like him – John Robertson once said to him: 'I think you're a brilliant manager, but if you walked into a pub, I'd walk straight out.'

His motivational tactic of selective rudeness was never likely to work with the group of star players at Leeds in the same way as it did at Derby and Forest. At those clubs the players had mostly achieved their first successes in their careers under Clough's management. The Leeds players rebelled against him, and the board, aware of the player discontent, sacked Clough after just 44 days in charge. Johnny Giles, Leeds player from that era, says of Clough's short reign:

> ❝We were mature, intelligent adults as well as experienced footballers and his rudeness backfired on him. It was just silly mind games that impressed nobody ... He got rid of himself, not the players. You could tell he was a bright guy, but where was the common sense? Why all the calculated rudeness?❞

It could also be said that Clough's style of man management is less suited to the modern era, as footballers have become more empowered as a result of increased social status and higher salaries and people in general are now less inclined to accept rudeness or bullying from a manager. Gary McAllister, then at Leicester, was offered a contract at Forest in 1989, towards the end of Clough's career, but pulled out of the proposed transfer purely because he thought Clough had been excessively rude to him during the negotiations.

Clough may well have still been in alignment with the culture of Nottingham Forest, not least because it had been created by him. Nevertheless, that culture was out of kilter with the prevailing culture of the industry. The Forest culture and Clough had become anachronisms in the industry. In business this phenomenon is best observed where the founding partners of companies are moved aside because they are perceived as compromising the brand they themselves have created. The upheaval at Saatchi & Saatchi in 1994 and 1995 when the Saatchi brothers themselves were usurped was a classic example.

We have spoken in Chapter 2 about the need for managers to be aligned with the brand of the club. Of course, both the manager and the club can change their brand in order to bring about such alignment, but it is preferable to look for a match. The appointment of Jeffrey Immelt as Jack Welch's successor, for example, was clearly an attempt to match the manager to the brand. However, it must also be recognized that if a company's brand is already irreparably damaged, the board may want the incoming manager to change the brand. Either way, brand alignment is never an easy task and its importance must never be underestimated. When that consummate stock player, Warren Buffett, paid £572 million to acquire the clothing group Fruit of the Loom, he said: 'We've agreed to buy Fruit of the Loom for two major reasons: the strength of the brand and the managerial talent of [COO] John Holland.' In other words, the alignment of the brands.

TEAM MANAGEMENT

Despite the obvious value of such factors as the way in which the manager treats the players, they still have to go out and actually play. The way in which they do so is analogous to the product processes of most businesses. How is the product – in football's case, winning matches – delivered? In football it is about the interaction between the players and the system of play selected by the managers. Although the great motivators publicly eschew the significance of tactics, in reality they must acknowledge that without a winning system, nothing would be won.

How, then, do managers select a playing system and a tactical approach? George Burley (Ipswich Town) gave an interesting take on this: 'If I could choose any players in the world to make up my team I would go for a 4–4–2,' he said. When asked why, he said: 'It gives the greatest number of attacking options with the most solid defensive shape.' In the FA Coaches Association Journal, *Insight* (Issue 4, Vol. 4, Autumn 2001) Derek Fazakerley, a former coach of Premiership side Blackburn, agreed with Burley:

> **"**4–4–2 gives you good balance right across the pitch, enabling you to double up on the wide players when you are both attacking and defending, providing good support. You can also supplement the midfield if necessary with a withdrawn striker.**"**

In a later edition of the FA journal (Issue 1, Vol. 5, Winter 2001) Dave Bassett also extols the virtues of 4–4–2:

> **"**It's the best way of covering space on the pitch and is very adaptable in that it can be used as an attacking formation and can also be put to good effect when you are forced on the defensive.**"**

Sven Goran Eriksson is also a devotee of the 4–4–2 system, as is Alex Ferguson, despite his fiddling in the early stages of the 2001/02 season. The Brazilians of 1958, 1962 and 1970 used a variant of 4–4–2, as did the Real Madrid side of the 1960s and the great Milan sides of the 1990s. Even the famous 4–3–3 used by Ramsey in 1966 effectively played with only two front players (Hurst and Hunt) and until very late in the World Cup campaign Ramsey used John Connelly and Terry Paine as traditional wingers.

Even if our observations about 4–4–2 are correct, what relevance can that possibly have to business? The relevance is that it demonstrates the importance of understanding the basic principles of the game, be it business or football. It also shows the importance of having a system of play (work/operation) that is flexible enough to exploit the opposition's weaknesses and resist their strengths. The 4–4–2 system does that. By employing players in virtually permanent wide positions when you have possession, the opposition will be stretched from side to side, enabling penetrative passes to be played between defenders. By pulling the wide players in from the flanks when the opposition is in possession you can present two banks of four defenders between the ball and your goal.

The shape of the team is, therefore, able to expand and contract, almost instantaneously, in relation to the possession of the ball. Of course, this demands a huge work rate from the players but it is also hugely effective. A business that can adopt a system as sensitive to playing conditions (the market, for instance) as the 4–4–2 system will be in a strong competitive position. Businesses must, therefore, look for an operational system which is based on fundamental principles and not merely reactive to contemporary symptoms. Only by understanding basic principles is it possible to exploit that knowledge to best advantage.

> A business that can adopt a system as sensitive to playing conditions as the 4–4–2 system will be in a strong competitive position.

However, if we refer back to George Burley's comment, he also said that without the right players it was sometimes not possible to play your preferred system. This is the conundrum that Eriksson faces with England. The dearth of left-sided attacking players is a problem the manager must solve in order to win anything. He must decide whether natural left-sided players like, for example, Alan Thompson of Celtic, offer more to the team than converted right-sided players such as Nick Barmby and Emile Heskey. It is our view that balance, in football and business, is more important than individual prowess. The question is not whether Emile Heskey is a better *player* than Alan Thompson but whether Emile Heskey is a better *left-sided attacking player* than Alan Thompson in relation to the needs of the team. At the time of writing Eriksson is still struggling with this issue.

In business, as in football, the *balance* of the team is essential to its success. Sacrificing balance to accommodate individuals or even groups of individuals is dangerous at best, disastrous at worst.

Lesson

Go for the system of operations which permits the greatest sensitivity and flexibility to the environment and the market.

An A–Z of the greatest British managers

MATT BUSBY

Appointed as manager of Manchester United in 1945 at the age of 36. Many of his great young side, nicknamed the 'Busby Babes', perished in the Munich air disaster of 1958. He rebuilt the team and United won the European Cup under his management in 1968, the first English team to do so. He also won five League Championships and the FA Cup twice at United.

HERBERT CHAPMAN

The first of the great British football managers. He created sides which won the League Championship three times in a row for Huddersfield (1924/26) and Arsenal (1933/35). The first manager to win the Championship with two different teams. He also won the FA Cup at both Huddersfield and Arsenal.

BRIAN CLOUGH

Won his first League Championship as a manager with Derby County in 1972, at the age of 37. After his infamously short and disastrous spell at Leeds United, he managed to improve on his remarkable feat at Derby by leading the similarly unfashionable Nottingham Forest, who were languishing in Division Two on his arrival in 1975, to a League Championship and the European Cup twice within five years.

STAN CULLIS

Appointed as manager of Wolverhampton Wanderers in 1948 at the age of 31. By 1960, his teams had won the League Championship three times and the FA Cup twice. Wolves had not won the League Championship before his arrival and have not won it since his departure.

ALEX FERGUSON

As manager of Aberdeen, he managed to break the dominance of the 'Old Firm', Rangers and Celtic, within Scottish football. In eight seasons, his team won the Scottish League Championship three times (and this at a club which had only won the league once before), the Scottish Cup four times and the European Cup Winners Cup, before he was appointed as manager of Manchester United in 1986. His United teams have won the League Championship seven times, the FA Cup four times, the European Cup and the European Cup Winners Cup.

BERTIE MEE

Promoted from physiotherapist to manager at Arsenal in 1966, after the team had been struggling in mid-table in Division One for several seasons. In 1971, his team won the League Championship and the FA Cup double.

BILL NICHOLSON

Became manager of Tottenham Hotspur in 1958. Within five years, his team had won the League Championship and FA Cup double (1961), the FA Cup (1962) and the European Cup Winners Cup (1963). Spurs also won the UEFA Cup under his management, in 1972.

BOB PAISLEY

Was the long-time assistant to Bill Shankly at Liverpool before he took over as manager upon Shankly's retirement in 1974. During his nine-year reign, his teams won the League Championship six times, the European Cup three times and the UEFA Cup.

ALF RAMSEY

Took over at Ipswich Town in 1955 at the age of 35. Ipswich were then in Division Three (south). In 1962, Ipswich won the First Division League Championship for the first and only time in their history.

Ramsey's success soon earned him the position of England manager. England won their first and only World Cup under Ramsey in 1966.

DON REVIE

Appointed as manager of Leeds United in 1961 at the age of 33, when the club was struggling in Division Two. During his spell as manager, Leeds won the League Championship twice, the FA Cup and the European Fairs Cup twice. He was appointed as manager of England in 1974.

BILL SHANKLY

Became manager of Liverpool in 1959 when the club was in Division Two. Under his management, the club won the League Championship three times, the FA Cup twice and the UEFA Cup. He also built the foundations on which Bob Paisley would then capitalize.

JOCK STEIN

The greatest manager in the history of Scottish league football. Appointed as manager of Glasgow Celtic in 1965, his teams won ten Scottish League Championships (including nine in succession), eight Scottish Cups and the European Cup before his departure in 1978.

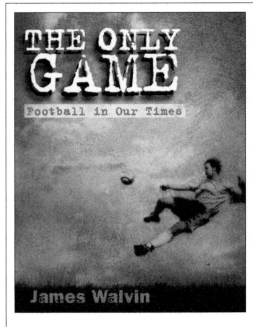

'Book of the Week . . . a well-researched yet polemic account of football's evolution, politics and future.'
Times Higher Education Supplement

'offers plenty of informed comment'
Andrew Longmore, *Independent*

'For an intelligent and thought-provoking overview . . . this is hard to beat.'
Andy Potts, *Fulham and Hammersmith Chronicle*

THE ONLY GAME
James Walvin
ISBN 0582-50577-1

This is the biography of football and it is an amazing story. From village mobs kicking around an inflated pig's bladder 600 years ago to the most lucrative and popular sport in the world, football has become a vast global business whose employees are multi-millionaires with celebrity status.

Yet, little more than a decade ago, English football was in a state of terminal decline. What has happened to change football so dramatically?

THE ONLY GAME follows the changing face of football against the background of changes to England as a whole.

Packed with the most telling photographs of the football era, THE ONLY GAME covers in detail the years of violence, racism, and ultimately tragedy, that brought English football to its knees, and how the game was saved.

visit our website at **www.history-minds.com**

Appendix B

Biblography: business references

Adair, J. (1988) *The Action Centred Leader*, Industrial Society Press.

Aldred, C. (2000) 'Stress levels growing', *Business Insurance*, 13 March.

Anonymous (2000a) 'Man U on the menu', *Director*, July.

Axelrod, E., Handfield-Jones, H. and Welsh, T. (2001) 'The war for talent, part two', *The McKinsey Quarterly*, No. 2.

Belbin, R.M. (1981) *Management Teams*, Butterworth-Heinemann.

Buckingham, M. and Coffman, C. (1999) *First, Break All the Rules*, Simon and Schuster.

Butler, T. and Waldroop, J. (1999) 'The art of retaining your best people', *Harvard Business Review*, September/October.

Capelli, P. (2000) 'A market-driven approach to retaining talent', *Harvard Business Review*, January/February.

Chambers, E., Foulon, M., Handfield-Jones, H., Hankin, S. and Michaels, E. (1998) 'The war for talent', *The McKinsey Quarterly*, No. 3.

Charan, R. (1999), 'Why CEOs fail', *Fortune*, 21 June.

Collins, J. (2001) *Good to Great*, Random House.

Cooper, T. (1999), 'Field of vision', *Director*, August.

Davidson, A. (1995) 'The Andrew Davidson interview: Gerry Robinson', *Management Today*, June.

de Geus, A. and Senge, P. (1997) *The Living Company*, Harvard Business School.

Dixon-Kheir, C. (2001) 'Supervisors are key to keeping young talent', *HR Magazine*, January.

Drucker, P. (1988) 'The coming of the new organisation', *Harvard Business Review*, January.

Drucker, P. (2001) 'The next society: a survey of the near future', *The Economist*, November 3.

Garten, J. (2001) *The Mind of the CEO*, Penguin.

Goleman, D. (1995) *Emotional Intelligence*, Bloomsbury.

Handfield-Jones, H. (2000) 'How executives grow', *The McKinsey Quarterly*, No. 1.

Katzenbach, J. and Smith, D. (1998) *The Wisdom of Teams*, McGraw-Hill.

Keidel, R. (1985) *Game Plans*, E.P. Dutton.

Lauterbach, B., Vu, J. and Weisberg, J. (1999) 'Internal vs external successions and their effect on firm performance', *Human Relations*, December.

Loch, C., Huberman, B. and Stout, S. (2000) 'Status competition and performance in work groups', *Journal of Economic Behaviour and Organisation*, September.

Loehr, J. and Schwartz, T. (2001) 'The making of the corporate athlete', *Harvard Business Review*, January.

Lorenz, A. (1997) 'Worth more together ... or apart', *Management Today*, November.

Mintzberg, H. (1998) 'Covert leadership: notes on managing professionals', *Harvard Business Review*, November/December.

Pfeffer, J. (2001) 'Fighting the war for talent is hazardous to your organisation's health', *Organisational Dynamics*, Spring.

Rappaport, R. (1993) 'To build a winning team: an interview with head coach Bill Walsh', *Harvard Business Review*, January/February.

Rice, M. (2000) 'Age of the flex exec', *Management Today*, August.

Rothenburg, R. (2001) 'Arie de Geus: the thought leader interview', *Strategy and Business*, No. 2.

Senge, P. (1993) *The Fifth Discipline*, Random House Publishing.

Tulgan, B. (2000) *Managing Generation X: How to Bring Out the Best in Young Talent*, W.W. Norton.

Tulgan, B. (2001) *Winning the Talent Wars*, Nicholas Brealey.

Verespej, M. (1999) 'Uninspiring leadership', *Industry Week*, 1 February.

Bibliography: football references

Adams, T. (1999), *Addicted*, HarperCollinsWillow.

Allen, M. (2000) *Jimmy Greaves*, Virgin.

Bale, B. *Bremner! The Legend of Billy Bremner*, Andre Deutsch.

Bowler, D. (1996) *Shanks: The Authorised Biography of Bill Shankly*, Orion.

Bowler, D. (1998) *Winning Isn't Everything. A Biography of Sir Alf Ramsey*, Orion.

Buckley, A. and Burgess, R. (2000) *Blue Moon Rising: The Fall and Rise of Manchester City*, Milo.

Campbell, T. and Potter, D. (1998) *Jock Stein: The Celtic Years*, Mainstream.

Clough, B. (1995) *Clough*, Corgi.

Dunphy, E. (1991) *A Strange Kind of Glory*, Heinemann.

Eriksson, S.-G., Railo, W. and Matson, H. (2001) *On Football*, Carlton.

Ferguson, A. (1999) *Managing My Life*, Hodder and Stoughton.

Graham, G. (1995) *The Glory and the Grief*, Andre Deutsch.

Holden, J. (2000) *Stan Cullis: The Iron Manager*, Breedon.

Hopcraft, A. (1970) *The Football Man*, Sportsmans Book Club.

James, G. (1993) *Football with a Smile: The Authorised Biography of Joe Mercer OBE*, ACL and Polar.

Keith, J. (1999) *Bob Paisley: Manager of the Millennium*, Robson.

Kelly, S. (1997) *Fergie: The Biography of Alex Ferguson*, Headline.

Kelly, S. (1997) *Bill Shankly*, Virgin.

Lambert, C. (1995) *The Boss*, Pride of Place (UK).

Lovejoy, (1998) *Bestie*, Pan.

Marquis, M. (1970) *Sir Alf Ramsey: Anatomy of a Football Manager*, Arthur Barker.

McIlvanney, H. (1994) *McIlvanney on Football*, Mainsteam.

Miller, D. (1971) *Father of Football: The Story of Sir Matt Busby*, Pavilion.

Mourant, A. (1990) *Don Revie: Portrait of a Footballing Enigma*, Mainstream.

Murphy, P. (1993) *His Way: The Brian Clough Story*, Pan.

Rogan, J. (1989) *The Football Managers*, Queen Anne Press.

Stam, J. (2001) *Head to Head*, Collins Willow.

Studd, S. (1998) *Herbert Chapman Football Emperor*, Souvenir Press.

Taylor, R. and Ward, A. (1996) *Kicking and Screaming: An Oral History of Football in England*, Robson Books.

White, J. (1994) *Are you watching Liverpool? Manchester United and the 93/94 Double*, Heinemann.

Williams, J., Long, G. and Hopkins, S. (eds) (2001) *Passing Rhythms*, Berg.

Index